Baltimore at ten and got here
at twelve to day. as I am w
-iting I can hear [...] of
cannon. in the direction [...]gton
they have had a very hard battle o
the old battle ground of Bulls R.
the Rebels got badly licked the Re[b]
Gen. Ewell was killed and Jackson
wounded and they say taken
Jackson prisoner. the boys all feel
well and are all well but Frank
Osburn and Charles Wade they are i
the Hospital they are not very
sick but are not able to do milita[ry]
duty. the climate is good it has
not ben as warm here yet as i[t]
was in Binghamton. our water is
good but warm. the Col says

Dear Friend Amelia

Dear Friend Amelia

The Civil War letters of
Private JOHN TIDD

MARY JORDAN & JOYCE HATCH
with RONALD E. OSTMAN & HARRY LITTELL

Published in 2011 by
SIX MILE CREEK PRESS
902 Giles Street
Ithaca, New York 14850

Layout, design, and contemporary photography by Harry Littell
Copy editing by Alan Littell
Produced by Della R. Mancuso, Mancuso Associates, Inc.
Printed by Capital Offset Company, Inc.
Bound by Acme Bookbinding
Typeset in Adobe Garamond Pro

John Tidd's letters are held in the collection of Mary Jordon
unless otherwise noted in the text.

LIBRARY OF CONGRESS CONTROL NUMBER 2010934609
ISBN 978-0-615-39520-3

Printed in the United States of America
First edition

About This Book

THE CIVIL WAR is one of the most written about and debated of American historical periods. *Dear Friend Amelia* does not introduce new theories about the war and its historical era, but rather presents the first-hand accounts of one young soldier, prefaced by and juxtaposed against historical context.

John Tidd's letters are transcribed verbatim, with grammatical errors, inconsistent spellings, occasional lack of conventional paragraphing and sentence structure, and sometimes expressing points of view that have since become politically incorrect. John often used the term "nigger," which was common at the time.

Text and reference notes appear in "sidebars" adjacent to the letters and illustrations. Once a reference has been cited in full, subsequent debts to that source are expressed as author's last name, shortened title, and page location.

We have attempted to create a visually interesting book, citing original sources and dates for images whenever possible. Included are illustrations ranging from romantically sentimental to grisly and brutally realistic, in keeping with John's perceptions of soldiering and war at various times during his service. Some of what we have included will be familiar to persons knowledgeable about the Civil War, while other visuals are presented for the first time. The materials vary from images that appeared during and shortly after the war to contemporary photographs of Civil War artifacts and locations mentioned in the text. Many of the historical photographs and lithographs have been cropped to draw attention to particular details.

Table of Contents

Prologue

In 1972, author Mary Jordan first glanced upon the following century old lines, inked by a graceful hand on yellowed army issue stationary, in a cache of recently discovered letters:

> *Dear Friend,*
> *... I am anxious to go and help put down this*
> *Rebellion, the greatest Rebellion the world ever saw*
> *& the most wicked. For two years Jeff & his minions*
> *have spread terror and desolation throughout the land,*
> *but I trust their career is about ended. I wish I could*
> *just go down and help Gen. Hooker take Richmond.*

Captivated, Mary continued to read, recognizing the names of local villages, famous generals, and historic battles. At that instant, Mary determined to devote herself to researching and publishing the story of the young soldier who penned the letters.

The book that has grown out of this effort, *Dear Friend Amelia,* is largely a collection of John Eliza Tidd Jr.'s surviving letters describing his Civil War experiences as a soldier in Company B of the 109th New York Volunteers from July 1862 through October 1865. This story documents John's affection and regard for Amelia Haskell, the young woman who was always in his thoughts back home in the small hamlet of Rawson Hollow, two miles from the larger bustling village of Speedsville, in central New York State.

John was born in 1839 in Ohio to John Tidd Sr. and Elisa Tidd. His sister Minerva was born in Ohio in 1844. His sister Armenia was born in 1846 at Caroline Center, in upstate New York. Their mother died shortly thereafter, when John was seven years old and Minerva two. John spent much of his early adulthood in Rawson Hollow, located approximately halfway between Ithaca and Binghamton.

Private John Tidd Jr., of Company B, the 109th New York Volunteers, c. 1862. Tintype. Collection of Mary Jordan.

The Speedsville stage, c. 1860s. Collection of Mary Jordan.

Rawson Hollow was named for Lyman Rawson, who built a cabin on West Owego Creek in 1802. Rawson was ambitious. He built a tavern, the Rawson Hollow Inn, about 1811. Rawson Hollow had mills and shops typical of small settlements of the era. It was a busy region, with traffic moving north from nearby Speedsville to the Catskill Turnpike, now called Route 79. The Rawson Hollow Inn became a stage stop.

Like many small settlements in the 1860s, Speedsville was mostly self-sufficient. The residents raised their own meat and vegetables. They had feed, grist, and lumber mills, two general stores, a cheese and butter factory, tin shop, blacksmith's shop, hotel, millinery shop, post office, school, soap factory, woodworking shop, wagon and carriage manufacturing shop, harness and repair shop, carpenters and joiners, shoe and boot makers, resident doctor, newspaper, three churches, and a bowling alley, making it unnecessary for residents to travel far from home. There was a lively social life, too. The churches were a center for various activities and residents also gathered for park picnics, box socials, dances, horseshoe games, ballgames, horse races, and in the winter, sledding, sleigh rides, and pond skating. If they wished, they could take lessons in penmanship, music, and dancing.

Amelia, John's dear friend, was born to Peter and Myra Olney Haskell on July 22, 1842. She had seven brothers and five sisters. The Haskell family lived in Lower Jenksville, New York, where Peter worked as a cobbler (Speedsville was called Upper Jenksville until the name was changed in 1835). After leaving home, Amelia lived and worked at George and Janette Williams's home, in Rawson Hollow.

Prior to his enlistment, on July 31, 1862, John also boarded with the Williamses. John worked as a cooper nearby, making wooden casks (firkins) at the Owens and Brothers Cooperage. Firkins, made from spruce or fir, could hold 50 pounds, usually of butter or soap.

During John's enlistment, his father suffered from heart disease and rheumatism. Throughout his military service, John sent money for his father's care to George Nixon Jr., below, who owned a combined house and cobbler's shop in Speedsville, where he plied his trade as a shoemaker and served as Justice of the Peace.

John's Regiment, the 109th New York Volunteers, guarded the railroad, bridges, and telegraph lines from Baltimore, Maryland, to Washington, D.C., from September 1862 to mid-January 1864. Then, after more than 15 months of guard duty, the 109th received orders to deliver new volunteers and conscripts to their assigned regiments at the front and to help guard Confederate prisoners in transit.

In April 1864, the 109th became part of the 1st Brigade, 3rd Division, 9th Army Corps, Army of the Potomac. As the Army moved southward toward Richmond, Virginia, the 9th Corps saw action in 18 separate battles, skirmishes, and assaults, including the Battles of the Wilderness, Spotsylvania Court House, Ny River, North Anna River, Totopotomoy Creek, and Cold Harbor, followed by constant trench warfare during the Siege of Petersburg through April 2, 1865. Petersburg was an important railroad and supply center located south of the Confederate capital of Richmond.

That John's Civil War story can be told is due to a curious set of circumstances.

Many years after the Civil War, Amelia's daughter, Clara, and Clara's husband, Dr. William Gallagher II, lived in an upstate New York house in Slaterville Springs. In 1972, the subsequent owners, Herman and Maggie Moesch, discovered letters, documents, and other items of historical interest from the 1800s in a secret room. A small alcove was located under the stairs leading to the second story. The Moesch's granddaughter, Heidi, had fallen against the back wall of this alcove while playing with friends. At first she thought she had crashed through the wall, but soon found she had sprung open a door whose hinges were concealed on the inside. The Moesches found a trove of keepsakes, some of which once belonged to Amelia more than a hundred years earlier. A beautiful wedding gown was draped over several cardboard boxes. Simple but elegant, the dress had intricate detail on the bodice and tiny buttons adorning the sleeves and neckline. The delicate fabric, discolored and fragile from years of accumulated dust, disintegrated when handled. The boxes contained family photographs, a book of Freemasonry dated 1860, ceremonial Masonic artifacts including a cap and apron, newspaper obituaries, wills, land deeds, a genealogy of the Williams family of Rawson Hollow, and a Confederate belt buckle.

Rawson Hollow bridge, near Speedsville, New York, c. 1860s. Collection of Mary Jordan.

Further exploration yielded a file of letters in a small black-and-gold-trimmed metal box. There were 35 letters from John Tidd to Amelia as well as a pair of photographs of the two young people. The box also contained more than 50 letters to Amelia from family and friends—but none from Amelia herself.

Author Mary Jordan lived with the Moesch family in the Slaterville Springs home during her teenage years until her marriage. Knowing Mary's love of history, Maggie Moesch gave her the letters shortly after their discovery. Mary enlisted the aid of her sister, Joyce Hatch, to ground each letter with relevant historical context. Now, after almost 40 years of intermittent research, Mary and Joyce have tracked down clues to help solve some of the letters' riddles. The authors discovered five more of John Tidd's letters and his diary at the town historian's office at Berkshire, a community a few miles from Speedsville, plus eight additional "Dear Friend Amelia" letters—three in the U.S. Army Heritage and Education Center, at Carlisle, Pennsylvania, and five in a private collection.

The family home of George and Janette Williams, in Rawson Hollow, where John and Amelia boarded. The Williamses' house was built in 1844 by George's father, Judge David Williams. It was located near the judge's home on West Creek Road, just beyond the Rawson Hollow School, c. 1860s. Collection of Mary Jordan.

John's letters to Amelia are sometimes poetic and affectionate, sometimes angry and disillusioned. They provide revelations about guard duty, combat, desertions, disease, and drunkenness, as well as descriptions of places and historical events. His letters and the accompanying text tell one soldier's story of the Civil War.

Call to Arms

The newspapers, the gossip of the village, his own picturings, had aroused him to an uncheckable degree. They were in truth fighting finely down there. Almost every day the newspapers printed accounts of a decisive victory.

—Stephen Crane, *The Red Badge of Courage*, 1895

BOOM! BOOM! Boom! Boom! All afternoon on July 12, 1862, the Speedsville cannon blasted away. The booming resonated for miles around, echoing through the small hamlets and farms nestled within the long valley and forested hills stretching from Caroline Center to nearby Owego. People within a seven-mile radius of Speedsville clearly heard the cannon's explosions.

The cannon's roar announced a greatly anticipated Speedsville social gathering. New York State Assemblyman Benjamin F. Tracy, elected on the Unionist ticket in 1861 and closely associated with the Republican Party, had scheduled an important Civil War meeting. A few citizens living in the outlying areas may have been unaware of the meeting and perhaps wondered if the noise was thunder. However, the mid-July sky was clear. If they were curious enough to ask, neighbors soon set them straight on what was happening—Tracy was seeking able-bodied men, two regiments' worth, to bolster the war effort.

Not everyone in Speedsville and environs had a comprehensive idea of what had happened to the Northern armies after April 12, 1861, when Southern secessionists shelled Fort Sumter, South Carolina. The first wave of eager volunteers, who filled President Abraham Lincoln's call for 75,000 soldiers to quell the rebellion, had obligations to serve from only three months to two years. In the spring of 1861 the populations of the North, fighting for the Union's preservation, and the South, fighting for recognition as a newly declared indepen-

Many Speedsville area settlers were strongly patriotic veterans of the Revolutionary War. Veteran Abner Merrick brought a Revolutionary War cannon home to Speedsville. It was fired during celebrations and to announce important community gatherings.

Illustration created from the cover of Charles Carleton Coffin, *Drum-Beat of the Nation* (New York: Harper & Brothers, 1888).

dent nation, tended to think that war—if it came—would be of short duration, perhaps settled in a single battle. By July 1, 1862, however, Lincoln realized that the North faced a long war, having witnessed both defeat and triumph in battles. He signed an order calling for 300,000 volunteer soldiers to serve three years.

Those who thought the rebellion would be easily quashed were mistaken. Armies from North and South met July 21, 1861, at Manassas Junction, near Washington, D.C., in the First Battle of Bull Run (Confederates called the battle "First Manassas"). The South routed the North after General Thomas J. Jackson and his Virginians stopped the advance of Major General Irvin McDowell's green Union soldiers, who eventually panicked and fled north and eastward toward Washington, thus earning Jackson his nickname, "Stonewall."

In August, Federal armies fought and lost the Battle of Wilson's Creek, Missouri. Union Brigadier General Nathaniel Lyon died in this battle. A segment of the Missouri State Militia, fighting on the Confederate side, moved on to Lexington, Missouri, and forced the surrender of the Federal garrison on September 20, winning the spoils of victory, including supplies, ammunition, and weapons. However, that month Union naval ships and transports captured Fort Hatteras, in North Carolina. In September, Confederates entered Kentucky. October saw the Battle of Ball's Bluff, Virginia, in which "The Potomac, here, was red with the blood of the Union slain." In November, the Union Navy captured two forts on Port Royal Sound, South Carolina, during the Hilton Head campaign. In February 1862, Union Brigadier General Ulysses S. Grant, assisted by gunboats, captured Forts Henry and Donelson, in Tennessee. The Battle of Pea Ridge, in Arkansas, was waged with the forces of Union General Samuel Curtis decisively defeating Major General Earl Van Dorn's Confederates in early March. In the same month, the USS *Monitor* fought the South's *Virginia* to a draw near Hampton Roads, Virginia.

Dr. James Moore, *A Complete History of the Great Rebellion; Or, the Civil War in the United States, 1861-1865* (Philadelphia: Quaker City Publishing House, 1867) 81.

General George B. McClellan's Army of the Potomac began its siege of Yorktown, Virginia, in April. The Battle of Shiloh was fought, in Tennessee, in early April, with General Grant holding the field. In late April, Confederates surrendered New Orleans, Louisiana, to Admiral David G. Farragut and his Gulf Expeditionary Force Navy. Soon thereafter, Baton Rouge and Natchez capitulated.

From March through May, "Stonewall" Jackson's men waged the Shenandoah Valley campaign and through calculated and mystifying strategies baffled and finally defeated Federal forces. His army captured large stores of war supplies, equipment, horses, and transportation vehicles. Also in late May, the Battle of Fair Oaks (also called "Seven Pines") began, in Virginia, but after much bloodshed neither side could be said to have won. From June 26 to July of 1862, a number of Virginia engagements, collectively named the "Seven Days Battles," were masterminded by the newly appointed General Robert E. Lee and his Confederate Armies of Northern Virginia. When the carnage ceased and bodies were counted, McClellan technically might have "won," but he had lost his taste for battle and ordered his forces to retreat to Harrison's Landing, on the James River, instead of pressing a counterattack as recommended by several on his staff. Thus, Lee is credited with driving McClellan's troops off the peninsula and away from Richmond, the Confederate capital.

By the time New York State had begun its July and August 1862 volunteer recruitment drives, in which Speedsville and nearby communities would play a role, many early Union recruits had found that army life wasn't as glamorous as they had thought. Northern soldiers were leaving the ranks as soon as the end of July 1861, with their obligations fulfilled, or were deserting. To replenish the ranks, Lincoln underscored the urgency of the situation. Clearly, the North would enact a draft if an insufficient number of volunteers enlisted.

Assemblyman Tracy, a prominent Owego, New York, law-

James M. McPherson, *Ordeal by Fire: The Civil War and Reconstruction* (New York: Alfred A. Knopf, 1982) 244-248.

Desertions during the war averaged about 10 percent for both Union and Confederate soldiers. Toward the end of the war, the desertion rate among Southerners was much higher. Arthur M. Schlesinger, Jr., Editor, *The Almanac of American History* (New York: G. P. Putnam's Sons, 1983) 283.

yer, organized army recruiting in Broome, Tioga, and Tompkins Counties at the request of New York Governor Edwin D. Morgan. According to *The Owego Gazette*, Tracy spearheaded the effort to raise two regiments of approximately 1,000 men each: the 109th and the 137th New York Volunteers. Tracy earned a commission as Colonel of the 109th on July 22, 1862, only 20 days after the President's order.

On July 12, 1862, Robert Hyde, working at the Temperance House in Speedsville, spent the day busily recruiting a company of men for the 109th. Although the recruitment meeting wasn't scheduled until 7 p.m., many gathered early to be on hand when Colonel N. W. Davis arrived on the afternoon stage from Owego.

The crowd congregated in the Speedsville Park while waiting for the evening's patriotic speeches, songs, and recruitment hoopla. In a holiday mood, many had packed picnic lunches. The "Speedsville Brass Band" usually could be counted upon to entertain the community from the park pagoda and almost all members were on hand for this occasion.

That evening, Colonel Davis, Hyde, and others spoke to the large crowd about the Civil War and the opportunities for men to serve in the Union Army. The question of slavery was not addressed, just as it was almost never mentioned in speeches at

President Lincoln wrote New York Governor Edwin D. Morgan: "If I had fifty thousand additional troops here now, I believe I could substantially close the war in two weeks. But time is everything; and if I get fifty thousand new men in a month, I shall have lost twenty thousand old ones during the same month, having gained only thirty thousand, with the difference between old and new troops still against me. The quicker you send, the fewer you will have to send. Time is everything." Roy P. Basler, Editor, *The Collected Works of Abraham Lincoln*, Volume 5, p. 296, Letter to Edwin D. Morgan, July 3, 1862.

The Temperance House and the Old Silk Hats Fox Hunting Club. Several Speedsville residents built the Temperance House in 1851. By 1862, the house was operating as a hotel and stage coach stop. The Sons of Temperance, the Masons, and others used the building for parties, meetings, dances, and social functions. *The Owego Gazette*, The Speedsville Temperance Hall. March 1, 1928.

The buildings, left to right, are the Speedsville School, probably built in 1823, the same time as the Universalist Church, the second building. To the right of the livestock shed is the Methodist Church, built in 1851 and dismantled in 1945. The park pagoda is in the right foreground and a woodshed is on the far right. The Speedsville Cemetery is behind the woodshed.

numerous war meetings throughout the country. The speakers emphasized that the war was being fought to preserve the Union rather than to abolish slavery. Many in the crowd that evening were familiar with slavery. First settlers in Tompkins and Tioga Counties had come from Maryland, Virginia, and the Carolinas, some bringing their slaves. By 1827, when slavery was formally abolished in New York State, most slaves already had been allowed to buy their freedom or had been set free. However, Hyde's father was remembered as a man who kept his slaves and mistreated them, even after the New York State freeing of the slaves. Although many men in upstate New York did not believe in slavery, abolition wasn't their foremost reason for joining the army.

The evening ended with Robert Hyde calling for volunteers to come forward and enlist, after reminding them of the $52 bonus. Not one man volunteered to join! The State of New York's $27 bounty and the Federal Government's $25 incentive failed to entice anyone to join the war effort on such short notice. Many potential recruits were farmers, either harvesting or planning to harvest their crops for the season, with the coming winter not far from their thoughts.

Later, as further inducement to fill New York's quota of 59,705 volunteers, more money was added. *The Owego Ga-*

President Lincoln did not publicly stress an end to slavery at this point in the war. On August 22, 1862, he stated in a letter to newspaper publisher Horace Greeley, "My paramount object … is to save the Union, and it is not either to save or to destroy slavery." However, he had already written a preliminary draft of the Emancipation Proclamation and had shared it with his Cabinet on July 22, 1862, in anticipation of the future. The Proclamation was published in Northern newspapers on September 23, 1862. Arthur M. Schlesinger Jr., editor, *Almanac*, 283-285.

zette reported on July 31, 1862: "A private, enlisting under the new call for volunteers, if the war should close within twelve months, would receive besides his regular rations and clothing, the following amount of money: state bounty $50; government advance bounty $27; one-month advance pay $13; pay per year $156; government bounty at close of war $75; rations $108; clothing, about $20. The total for one year's pay came to $449. In addition to the $449, all wounded and disabled, would receive a pension for life."

Many districts offered additional bounties and resolved that a set amount each month, raised by subscription and a special tax, would be paid to the soldiers' families while soldiers were in service.

Pressure and excitement were building. Many potential recruits had never traveled more than 20 miles from home. The promise of adventure, coupled with patriotism for country, the financial incentives, growing community support, the pro-enlistment newspaper articles and editorials, and above all the threat of a draft if the New York quota was not met, became the main inducements to join.

Robert Hyde held several additional war meetings in the nearby communities of Berkshire, Candor, Caroline, Nanticoke, Newark Valley, Owego, and Richford. War meetings were held by other recruiters throughout the State's 24th Senatorial District in an effort to raise the remaining nine companies of the 109th. There were substantial incentives for recruiters as well, who could earn as much as $4 for each recruit. Although Hyde's war meetings drew large crowds, by August 8, 1862, he had convinced only 20 men to sign their enlistment papers. John Tidd was one of the first in Speedsville to enlist in Hyde's Company B of the 109th. His enlistment papers, of July 31, 1862, state he was 23 years old when he signed to serve three years in the infantry. Eighteen of the 20 enlistees had enrolled from the Newark Valley area at a war meeting held there August 6, 1862. Hyde needed 80 more men to form a company.

The Owego Gazette, War Meeting. July 17, 1862. The *Gazette's* math appears too generous. The figure probably should be $436.

The draft was to be enacted August 15. If drafted, men would lose the right to choose their regiment and would not receive the financial incentives. General Order 108, issued August 14 stated: "After the 15th of this month bounty and advanced pay shall not be paid to volunteers for any new regiments, but only to volunteers for regiments now in the field and volunteers to fill up new regiments now organizing but not yet full. The draft for 300,000 militia called for by the President will be made on Wednesday, the 3rd day of September, and continue from day to day, until completed." United States, War Dep't., Record and Pension Office, War Records Office. *The War of the Rebellion.* Accessed, Cornell University "Making of America" http://cdl.library.cornell.edu/cgi-bin/moa, (hereafter referred to as *O.R.*) 380-381.

A lifelong resident and the son of a slave owner, Robert Hyde received his appointment as Captain of Company B of the 109th on August 9, 1862. On the same day, Captain Hyde met with his volunteers and potential recruits at the Berkshire House, a church located a short distance from the town of Berkshire. Seventy-one men signed their enlistment papers at that meeting, bringing the total to 91 enrolled in Company B of the 109th. Each company in the regiment consisted of one captain, one first lieutenant, one second lieutenant, one first sergeant, four sergeants, eight corporals, two musicians, one wagoner and an average of 80 privates.

The Owego Gazette, How Much Will You Give? July 31, 1862.

The Owego Gazette, Fill Up the Ranks. July 31, 1862.

On August 11, 1862, Captain Hyde and his new company met in Owego. The freshly enlisted men arrived by wagon, on horseback, or on foot. Train service for this rural region was not available until 1869. *The Owego Gazette*, under the headline of "Military" on August 14, 1862, described the men of the 109th marching through Owego on their way to the train station for transport to Camp Susquehanna, in Binghamton: "Captain Hyde's company came into town this forenoon (August 11) accompanied by the Speedsville Brass Band, on their way to headquarters at Binghamton. The boys seem to be alive with enthusiasm. Cheer after cheer for the good old flag rent the air as they passed through our streets."

In July and August of 1862, as the ranks of the new regiments of the 24th Senatorial District from Broome, Tioga and Tompkins Counties of New York, were filled, a regimental campground in Binghamton on the south side of the Rockbottom Bridge, over the Susquehanna River, was prepared to receive the volunteers. Camp Susquehanna looked like a military encampment by August 6, with tents and barracks erected for the soldiers expected to arrive shortly.

Broome Republican, Spirit of Tioga. August 6, 1862.

Company B joined other new companies. By August 20, the 107th, 108th, and the 113th New York Regiments had vacated Camp Susquehanna and were in Washington, D.C., or on their way.

The Erie Railroad made special accommodations to transport soldiers' families and friends to the Susquehanna Military Camp to witness ceremonies of August 25, 1862, just prior to the 109th Regiment's departure for Maryland. Mr. Hancock of Owego presented an American flag, purchased by Owego citizens, to the 109th after many district dignitaries made flowery speeches. Amelia Haskell was in the crowd of well-wishers.

The Broome Republican. War News. August 6, 1862.

Volunteers in the 109th came from varied backgrounds and ranged in age from 15 to 49, many of whom were well established in their occupations. In addition to the loss of family men in the home, the communities suffered the loss of their trades. The jobs of farmers, mechanics, shoemakers, store clerks, school teachers, blacksmiths, and tailors were passed on to wives, family members, or men remaining in the communities, or were not filled at all.

The Owego Gazette, War Meeting at Newark Valley. August 11, 1862.

The 109th Regiment left Camp Susquehanna for Annapolis Junction, Maryland, on Saturday, the 30th of August 1862. Private John Tidd was on a journey away from home for the first time in his young life. He and most of the men gathered in the railroad cars must have spent some time reflecting upon what their futures held. What were they to do in the Union Army? How much training would they receive? When would they be issued arms and other army provisions? Surely they wouldn't be expected to go immediately into battle ... or would they? John's

The Speedsville Brass Band, c. 1860s. Collection of Mary Jordan.

questions may have included: What will my new life hold? How will my father fare while I'm gone? Will the money I send home be enough to keep him in reasonable comfort and security? Who will take my job at the barrel factory? How will Speedsville change

with so many men gone? Will the mail get through so I can stay in touch with Amelia? Will I be courageous in battle? Will I survive?

These, and many more thoughts, must have occurred to him. The train chugged along, the wheels click-clacking over the rails, taking them away into parts unknown. The countryside began to change and he began to watch the scenery roll by. Some of the men were playing cards. More than one had smuggled liquor aboard and were misbehaving. Finally, confusion and exhaustion overcame him and he slept, while the train kept moving away from the known and the partially known toward the wholly unknown.

"Troops to the Front." Johnson, Ridpath, Morgan, Howard, Connor, Howard, & Gordon. *Campfire and Battlefield* (New York: Bryan, Taylor & Company, 1894) 38.

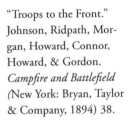

"The moment of parting with friends, and severing of ties hallowed by love and affection, which long years of intimacy and social relations had interwoven into every fibre of the human heart, came upon those about to leave—perhaps forever—with cold and chilling realities. Tears— scalding tears—flowed down many a cheek." *The Broome Republican*, August 30, 1862.

Life in a Camp

He had had the belief that real war was a series of death struggles with small time in between for sleep and meals; but since his regiment had come to the field the army had done little but sit still and try to keep warm.

—Stephen Crane, *The Red Badge of Courage*, 1895

Members of the 109th were sworn into Federal service on August 27, 1862. They shipped out only three days later, leaving Binghamton without firearms. They possessed only a few articles of clothing and other necessities. There was great urgency. General George Brinton McClellan, named Commander of the Division of the Potomac in July 1861 and then General-in-Chief of the Union Army in November of that year, had issued a frantic call for additional soldiers for Washington's defense. With the amassing of a large force of men, however, the government was struggling to supply regiments with clothes, weapons, canteens, haversacks, blankets, camp accoutrements such as cooking kettles, and suitable barracks. Edwin D. Morgan, Governor of New York, in a telegraph message to Edwin M. Stanton, Secretary of War, begged for more time. Stanton replied, "The emergency for troops here is far more pressing than you know or that I dare tell. Put all your steam on and hurry them up."

So, ill-provisioned and in not a little confusion, the 109th marched on Saturday, August 30, through Binghamton to the Erie Railroad Station. They boarded open cars and began their journey to Annapolis Junction, Maryland. After resting for a few hours in Elmira, New York, they again departed by rail, some in freight cars and the luckier ones in passenger cars. Again, crowds cheered them as they left for Williamsport, Pennsylvania. By early Sunday morning the 109th passed Harrisburg. They arrived in Baltimore around noon. Then they

O.R. V5 (14) 413.

Ledyard Bill, *Pen-Pictures of the War* (New York, 1866) cover.

marched to the relay house on the Washington Road, where they ate a supper of bread, cheese, meat, and coffee.

Unable to continue to Annapolis Junction until the next morning, the men spent the night on the depot's muddy floor and steps. Each company of about 80 men had been allotted only 20 blankets. It had rained most of the day. The men spent a miserable night. After a dry breakfast, they again boarded a train to travel 30 more miles, arriving about noon September 1 at Annapolis Junction, 20 miles from Washington.

Again, they were treated almost as heroes. The Ithaca, New York, band met them at the train station with a performance. The next morning they had dress parade for the first time. Again the Ithaca Band played rousing martial music, for which each company paid $22.

But the music and cheers were about spent. That afternoon, the soldiers began pitching the 13 tents issued each company. Shortly afterward, it started raining and the torrents didn't end until midnight. Sleeping six to seven men to a tent, they were able to keep reasonably warm if not dry. In the morning, only a small portion of rations was available. A foraging party left

Annapolis Junction. Library of Congress, Prints and Photographs.

As recounted by Jerome Woodbury of the 109th in a letter dated September 2, 1862.

camp to roam the countryside for provisions. They returned with peaches, apples, potatoes and melons.

But elsewhere, other Union Army soldiers were experiencing much more serious problems. While the 109th was in transit to Annapolis Junction, the Second Battle of Bull Run, near Manassas, Virginia, and Chantilly, only 20 miles from Washington, was fought at the end of August and in early September. The Rebels, led by General Robert E. Lee, General "Stonewall" Jackson, and Major General James Longstreet prevailed convincingly in both engagements and the Union forces were driven back to the heights of Centreville, Virginia. Historian James M. McPherson noted that the Rebels were poised for the kill, virtually on the outskirts of Washington. In the first week

Fortifications, Heights of Centreville, Virginia. Mathew Brady, 1862. Collection of Tioga County Historical Society, New York.

of September 1862, Confederates crossed the Potomac River in preparation for the Maryland campaign, a general invasion of the North toward Washington.

There was no love lost between Union generals at that time. General McClellan's Army of the Potomac gave precious little battle assistance to General John Pope, in command of the Union's Army of Virginia. Pope was unpopular with his troops and was thought to have moved too slowly in the debacle. As a result, he was relieved of his command. Pope's army was merged into the Army of the Potomac, and General McClellan, the "Little Mac" so popular with the troops, was appointed to head the Union Army in Washington's defense on September 2, 1862.

The Battle of South Mountain was fought on September 14. The Rebels held off Federal troops trying to get through a mountain pass to smash General Lee's divided forces, which were reconsolidating. The battle resulted in an estimated 4,500 casualties. Meanwhile, General Jackson's command took Harp-

James M. McPherson. *Battle Cry of Freedom: The Civil War Era* (New York: Oxford University Press, 1988) 532.

O.R. (24) 807.

Burying the dead of the battlefield of Antietam, Maryland. Alexander Gardner, 1862. Collection of Tioga County Historical Society.

ers Ferry, Maryland, on September 15, 1862, capturing both the Union garrison and a huge arsenal of equipment. The bloodiest single day of fighting of the entire Civil War took place two days later when McClellan's army met Lee's advancing force at Antietam, Maryland. Each side suffered more than 10,000 soldiers killed and wounded. Though Antietam was considered a draw, Lee's advance to the North was halted. On the 18th, Lee withdrew from his position and retreated across the Potomac into Virginia. McClellan had saved Washington, and Northern morale improved. However, President Lincoln was disappointed by McClellan's performance. He believed that McClellan's cautious and poorly coordinated actions in the field had forced the battle to a draw rather than crippling the Confederate forces. Accordingly, on November 5, the President replaced McClellan with Major General Ambrose E. Burnside, who took command of the Army of the Potomac.

Burnside proved incompetent. Despite overwhelming advantages, Burnside's forces were routed by Lee's army at Fred-

President Lincoln, General McClellan and staff on the battlefield of Antietam, Maryland. October 3, 1862. Mathew Brady. Collection of Tioga County Historical Society.

American Battlefield Protection Program (ABPP). CWSAC Battle Summaries.

ericksburg, Virginia, on December 13. There were more than two Federal casualties to General Lee's one (12,000 compared to 5,000). In late December, and in early January 1863, Union Major General William S. Rosencrans suffered 12,900 casualties, a third of his force. Confederate General Braxton Bragg suffered a similar percentage of casualties (11,700 men), making the Battle of Stones River (Murfreesboro, Tennessee) "the most deadly battle of the war in proportion to numbers engaged." While the Union advance toward Chattanooga's rail center was stymied, the Rebels inexplicably pulled back to a new position 25 miles south, thus saving the North from totally disastrous war news. President Lincoln was not fooled, however. He replaced Burnside. General Joseph Hooker became the head of the Army of the Potomac on January 25, 1863.

As for John Tidd and the men of the 109th, they would stay at Annapolis Junction, Maryland, and immediate vicinity for the next 15 1/2 months, guarding the Baltimore to Ohio Railroad from just outside Baltimore to Washington. Their responsibility in keeping it open to rail traffic was extremely important, since the line delivered troops and supplies to the Army of the Potomac. The 109th also guarded the telegraph line (built in 1847) that connected Washington south to Petersburg, Virginia, an important railroad center.

At the start of the war, the North possessed most of America's 50,000 miles of telegraph line, which had proved a boon to expanding industrial output due to the rapid communication possible over long distances. However, lines were easily cut. The Military Telegraph Corps was developed to string new lines as armies moved. The telegraph operators tapped out messages concerning

McPherson. *Battle Cry,* 582.

Cutting telegraph wires. Henry Davenport Northrop. *Queen of Republics* (Philadelphia: World Bible House) 752. For more on the telegraph see William C. Davis, Editor. *Fighting for Time. Volume Four of The Image of War 1861-1865* (New York:

the Army's locations, enemy movements and concentrations, supply needs, and hundreds of other vital bits of information, connecting generals and their staffs, President Lincoln and the Department of War, supply depots, and many other persons and locations. Operators, using portable field sending and receiving keys, powered their Morse codes with batteries in heavy horse-drawn wagons.

Back in Speedsville, although the soldiers were sorely missed, life went on much as before. In fact, many civilians prospered selling beef, butter, and cheese to brokers for the Army's use. Letters and news flowed from home to the regiment's companies and vice versa with reasonable regularity. John proved a better and more faithful writer than Amelia, judging from his occasional complaints and pleas for mail and news from home in letters to her. The men shared gossip from letters received, just as those back home were sharing the less private reports from Company B. Letters to the soldiers from Speedsville and other hometowns provided details regarding community social gatherings, such as dances, potluck suppers, holiday parties, hayride and sledding parties, picnics, and church activities. Some men, John included, occasionally wished they could be part of the fun. Their letters to Speedsville had precious little to report regarding entertainment, although there were some amusing and pleasant events and occasions, as John's letters, reproduced in full in his own voice, will now show.

Doubleday & Company, 1983)101-103; Phillip Shaw Paludan. "A People's Contest." The Union and Civil War 1861-1865 (New York: Perennial Library, 1989) 106.

Harry Boyer Diary, 1861-1865. Private collection of Clara Maynard, Speedsville, New York.

Unfortunately, and as noted in the prologue, no letters written by Amelia to John or to anyone else have been located. The only sense we can possibly have of Amelia's thoughts and personality is through the prism of John's letters to her, in which he discusses or responds to things she appears to have said in her letters to him.

Annapolis Junction. Sep 7 162

Dear. Friend. Amelia
                                This
pleasant afternoon as the sun
is fast declining in the west
I seat myself pen in hand to
Impart a few random thoughts
to one who is far away. though
the medium of this pen it
would be more satisfying to my
mind if I could have the pleasure
of spending a few hours with you
you must excuse me for not say
ing good bye to you I was very sorry
that I could not have the pleasure

Annapolis Junction. Sep 1st /62

Dear Friend Amelia,

    This pleasant afternoon as the sun is fast declining in the west, I seat myself, pen in hand, to impart a few random thoughts to one who is far away through the medium of this pen. It would be more satisfying to my mind if I could have the pleasure of spending a few hours with you. You must excuse me for not saying good bye to you. I was very sorry that I could not have the pleasure of your company a little longer but I could not leave my company. They made us stay there on parade till dark. Well, I must tell you how we get along and where we are. We started Satarday at eleven oclock and got to Williamsport [Pennsylvania] at nine in the evening. I saw Charley & Mr. Curtis. Charley thinks he will not go to war just now. The ladies treated us with pies and candles and every thing they had. Such a waveing of hankercheifs you never saw. The streets was lined with ladies & gentlemen.

John and Amelia, c. 1862. Letter and photographs from the collection of Mary Jordan.

We got to Baltimore about two oclock Sunday afternoon. We marched about two miles through the citty to another depot. We sleept on the depot steps all night. I was on guard for three hours there Monday morning. We left Baltimore at ten and got here at twelve to day. As I am writing, I can hear

the booming of cannon in the direction of Washington. They have had a very hard battle on the old battle ground of Bulls Run. The Rebels got badly licked, the rebel Gen Ewell was killed and Jackson wounded, and they say taken Jackson prisoner. The boys all feel well, and are all well but Frank Osburn and Charles Wade. They are in the hospital. They are not very sick but are not able to do military duty. The climate is good. It has not ben as warm here yet as it was in Binghamton. Our water is good but warm. The Col says we are going to stay here four weeks and form a Brigade and then go to Fortress Monroe [Virginia]. The Regt that is forming at Binghamton will be in the Brigade. Well, I must close and go to work. I

Dr. Sanford Hunt, surgeon of the 109th, wrote: "Each man has his own ideas of what is the chief end of a soldier. Some think that they came here to fight, and not to guard a 'dod-darned' railroad. The regiment on September 16th was cut up in six detachments, with so much picket and patrol duty that there was no drilling, and so much separation that we hardly know whether we belong to a regiment or to a mob." *Broome Weekly Republican*, October 8, 1862.

"Ladies and gentlemen greet the troops." Johnson, Ridpath, and others. *Campfire and Battlefield*, 38.

John's account regarding Confederate Generals Richard S. Ewell and Thomas J. ("Stonewall") Jackson is incorrect. "On the 30th of August, General John Pope met on the old battlefield of Bull Run against General [Robert E.] Lee. Exhausted, cut off from supplies, and overwhelmed by numbers, the shattered remains of the Union forces were driven back to the heights of Centreville, Virginia." *O.R.*

will give you the particulars of camp life in my next letter.
Give my respects to Mrs. Reed and all of my friends. I will
not send my love to anny of the girls, because I have not got
anny for them. I am well and hope these few lines will find
you enjoying the same blessing. Do as you would be done by,
that is to write soon. Do not forget to send you know what.
Now write as soon as you get this so that I can get it before
we go away from here. Write all the news and do not forget to
write. You must excuse all mistakes and poor writing for we
have not got a very good place to write. So good bye for the
present.

This is from your true friend and well wisher.

John Tidd

Soldiers' graves at Bull
Run, 1862. Mathew Brady.
Collection of Tioga County
Historical Society.

Annapolis Junction. Sep 14th /62

Dear Friend,

It was with pleasure that I perused your very kind letter which I received yestarday morning and was glad to hear you was all well and still standing up for the union. I am well and feel like fighting as much as ever. I wish you could have seen us last night lieing by the side of the railroad track in the dirt and cold enough to freeze a niger and again to day we are guarding the track, three to every telegraph pole. I told Mat Parker what you told me; he says he will endever to kill as many as two before they kill him, if not more. Mat and I tent together now and will be side by side on the Battle field. We are numberd of according to the height. Frank Taylor is not in the same rank and,

Mat [James M.] Parker and Frank [Francis M.] Taylor, both of Company B, were John's longtime friends.

therefore we cannot tent togather. Mat sends his best respects to you as an old friend of his. There is only two companys left here now, the Flag Company and ours. The Col says Company B will not go till he goes. He thinks we have got the best Company in the Regt. He and [Captain] Hyde are

Manassas, looking east, 1862. Mathew Brady. Collection of Tioga County Historical Society. John notes that at Annapolis Junction, the 109th guarded the tracks "three to every telegraph pole," similar to the scene in

togather most all the time. Hyde was quite sick yestarday. I have not heard from him this morning. We have got the soberist lot of men in the Regt you ever saw. They dont drink a drop nor gamble because they will not allow them to. They are a good deal more steady then they are to home. We have not seen anny thing of the box of cake yet that you sent us and presume never will, but we are just as thankful as though we had. You want to know if I have worked yet—yes I have and like it firstrate. I think you will have no business with me

Brady's photograph. Prior to the First Battle of Bull Run, many Union and Confederate officers and soldiers were overconfident, naïve, and untested, thinking of war as a grand adventure and lark. Some civilians also were clueless. Many Washingtonians, in a holiday mood, packed picnic lunches and traveled

in that line of business by the time I get back and also in the cooking line, not but what you are first rate in both branches, for I know you are, but Southern style is the best. But, never the less, I would like to step into your establishment some Sunday afternoon and get a warm meal got up by your own sweet self. I have not got home sick yet and do not intend to but would like to see you all very much but I had much rather stay and fight for you and our Countrys liberty then to be at home when our Country is in danger. You need not be afraid of the rebels comeing to Speedsville for you know I promised to keep them back. But, you are not the girl to be afraid of every scarcrow and especily of rebels. I think we will dine in Richmond before the forth if ever. But it seems hard to have to retreat backwards but our turn will come soon I hope when the rebels will be driven from the face of the earth. Our liveing is very good at presant but not as good as might be. We have Bread, Beans, Meat and Rice and Potatoes. So for any Southern beuty with dark eyes, I know of a Northern dark eyed beuty that I think more of then any Southern beuty that I have or shall come acrost. We sleep on the ground with nothing but ceder brush and some times nothing, but we sleep as sound as a log. I have slept a good many times out doors on the ground and can sleep as nice as a pin. Give my best respects to Mrs. Reed and Mary and all of the folks. Now you must be sure and send me your likeness the next time you write or I shall think you do not think much of me, for I should think all the world of it. Now please do. Write soon and write all the news. They all say that I am getting fat & do not know but I be. I certainly feel better than I have since last fall. Well, I must bring this letter to a close. Please excuse all mistakes and poor writing for the sake of the writer.

From your true and sincere friend,

John Tidd

Direct to same place that you did before.

across the river and headed along the railroad line toward Manassas Junction, Virginia, to witness what they thought would be a certain and glorious Union victory. Instead, they saw green Union troops tasting battle, becoming demoralized, and finally panicking and fleeing for their lives as rumors of disaster spread through the lines. Henry Steele Commager, Editor, *Illustrated History of the Civil War* (New York: Exeter Books, 1984) 153-154.

Annapolis Junction. Sep 26th /62

Dear Friend Amelia,

I received your most welcome letter last night and will,
with pleasure proceed at once to answer you. We are getting
along as well as can be expected under existing circumstances.
We are still here but do not know how long we shall be. The
whole Regt will be here to day. There is already five companys
here. The wether is getting quite cool. So cool at night that
we sleep cold in our tents and I tell you what it comes tough
enough to sleep out doors. We will have to have barracks
before long or we shall freeze. I beleive we have colder nights
here than you do there. I thought we was going south, but it
seems as if we was [going] north instead of south. I think we
can sleep on a pine knot by the time we get back, if we ever
do, and eat a raw dog. But, we can stand it if anny body can.
But, our liveing is good now to what I expected it would be.
My helth still continues to be good and so does that of the
Company generly. You want to know how we iron. We do not

iron, but if I had the tools to do it with, I could do it as well
as the best of them. I presume you would be happy to know
just how we live and what we do in camp life. Therefore, I
will with pleasure give you the particulars. We are called out
at sun rise to answer to rool call. We then have a cup of hot
coffee; then we have squad drill till halfpast seven; then we
have breakfast. At ten oclock we have battalion drill and drill
till noon with knap sacks, canteens and haversacks on. At two
we have company drill which lasts till four. We are out again
at five on dress parade, which lasts about an hour, then we
have supper. At nine, we have to again answer to our names.
Every light has to be blown out at half past nine. We are
on guard now once in three days. There is three reliefs. The
first comes on halfpast eight in the morning and are releived
halfpast ten and so on during twenty four hours so that each
man is on two hours and of four, which makes it quite easy
but rather tough to be waked up nights, but we have got used
to that. When we come of guard, we shoot our peices and the

Encampment of the Army.
Coffin, *Drum-Beat of the
Nation*, 183. By the middle
of September the weather
was cold with frequent rain
showers and caused much
suffering among the men.
Some companies of the
109th were still without
warm clothes, blankets
or barracks. Only in the
service a few weeks, many
of the soldiers already suffered from dysentery and
the measles. Most camp
grounds, vacated by former
regiments, were unsanitary
and their water supplies
tainted.

one that comes the closest to the mark is of duty for twenty four hours. Mat Parker was the lucky man the last time he was on guard. I have not shot but once yet at a mark, and then shot over, but close enough to kill a rebel. The rebels have ben drove out of Maryland but I think they got rather the best of the bargain with the capture of Harpers Ferry. Our loss in the late battles were probably about the same as theirs. As near as I can find out, it was a draw game. We could hear the roar of the cannons plain as you can hear the Speedsville cannon to Berkshire. One of our men have ben in the dungeon for the last ten days because he threatened to knock the guard down if he did not let him pass! My letters must have ben miscarried for they both ought to have ben there the Wednesday before you got yours. I do not know as

President Lincoln's Emancipation Proclamation was first printed in Northern newspapers on September 23. He signed General Order No. 139 on January 1, 1863, setting free all slaves in states still in rebellion. The Confederacy did not abide by the proclamation, and no slaves were set free. Its importance lies in the fact that it was a step in the direction of ending slavery, it encouraged slaves to rally to the North's cause, and it bolstered most abolitionists in the North and abroad. The Emancipation Proclamation was also an attempt by Lincoln to forestall Britain and France from recognizing the Southern Confederacy as a legitimate independent country. By playing the race card, Lincoln made it a foremost issue in the war. Foreign countries would hesitate before endorsing a country that condoned slavery. Bruce Catton, *The American Heritage Short History of the Civil War* (New York: Dell Publishing Co., Inc., 1965) 99-100, 106-108.

Abraham Lincoln's Emancipation Proclamation. Strobridge Lith. Co., c. 1888. Library of Congress, Prints and Photographs.

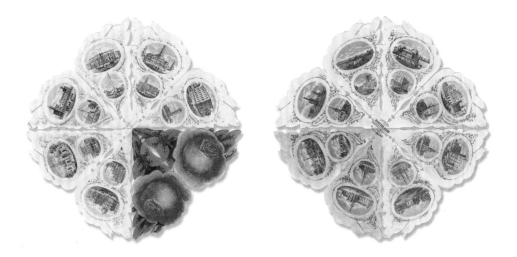

I care much wether I have the other girls pictures or not. But to please you and to get yours, I will ask them to send them or you may tell them for me. You had better beleive it keeps me pretty buisy writing when I am not on duty. This is the twenty seventh letter since I have ben here and have wrote to nineteen differnt persons and have received twelve in return. I have wrote so much that I cannot think of much to write. How do you like the Presidents Proclamation? I think it is good and so does most all of the soldiers. I have got the Rose of Baltimore that I am going to send to you. It will come in an envelope. It is a nice rose and pictures of the different buildings and streets in Baltimore. That largest street is the one we marched through. It is hard work to keep the day of the week. Sundays are like other days in war. Well I must close. Give my best respect to all the girls and to Mr. and Mrs. Reed. I do not know as you can read this. It is wrote so miserable but I am sure you will excuse me with these few lines. I will close hoping you will answer soon.

I remain as ever your true friend,

John Tidd
Annaplolis Junction

The Rose of Baltimore, front and back. Courtesy of Berkshire Historian's Office, New York.

Beltsville. October 12th 1862

My Dear Friend,

I now take the liberty to write a few lines, just as we are expecting to march to meet the enemy, to one who is far away but one who is ever near in my thoughts. I hope that after this unhappy rebellion is put down, I may return to you, my best of friends, and all of my old friends and schoolmates with all the honer that is due to a soldier who has gone at his Countrys call to defend her rights and her liberty. About an hour ago we was ordered to fall into line to receive forty rounds of catriges and was ordred to sleep on our arms to be ready to turn out at a minutes warning. In a few minutes after, the Col received a dispatch that the rebels was within eighteen or twenty miles from this place, Beltsville, and that they had just started a troop of Cavelry from Washington to be put under the command of Col Tracy, for the defence of this railroad at this and other points. We expect them here every moment! Telegraphic communication is out of between Poolesville and Harpers Ferry. There is great excitement in Washington. The rebels are again in Maryland. Wether they

On October 12, 1862, Colonel Tracy received a telegram from W. D. Whipple of the Eighth Army Corps: "Col. B. F. Tracy, Colonel: Keep well on your guard and be prepared to meet any raid upon the railroad from the enemy. Keep your troops well in hand. The railroad is cut at Monrovia, the other side of Monocaey, and the telegraph reported cut five miles beyond Poolesville." *O.R.* (63) 882.

Benjamin Franklin Tracy, left, and Isaac Swartwood Catlin, right. *History of Tioga, Chemung, Tompkins & Schuyler Counties, New York* (Philadelphia: Everts & Ensign, 1878) 177.

Cartridge belt (held 40 rounds) and examples of twisted paper powder cartridges. Collection of Michael Colella.

will again escape is to be seen but I hope we will be smart enough this time to prevent this escape! The Captain told us to night that if any of us was cowards he did not want us to come out of our tents if we was called on. He did not want any cowards in the ranks! I and twenty others went out on a scouting expidicion about two miles and back this forenoon. Our Company has got the inside track of the other Companys. We are the favorite Company of the Regt. We have more privileges then all the others & we have moved from where we was. We are now at Beltsville, thirteen miles from Washington in a very beautiful place. Well, I cannot write any more now for I am in a hurry. When I write again I will tell you all the particulars of our march and our place. Write without delay and a good long letter. I may be called up before morning. If I be, I will try and kill as many as two or three for you. Give my respects to all.

This from your true friend,

John Tidd

Direct to Beltsville, Prince George County, MD.

"Green" troops, imagining battle, often think in terms of personal bravery and courage, and inflicting damage and pain upon others. John and his friend Mat have done some bragging about their imagined future superhuman prowess and invulnerability in killing Confederates. Yet their captain may have taken some lessons from the First Battle of Bull Run. Faced with real battle for the first time, some soldiers fight and others take flight.

Beltsville. October 25th, 1862

Friend Amelia,

It is with pleasure that I avail myself of the opportunity presented this pleasant morning to answer your short but by no means unwelcome letter, which I received on the 31st. I was sorry to hear that you were going to leave Speedsville but do not blame you for wanting to see your sister [Sarah] & especially when she is not very well and needs the kind attention of a sister. I presume it will not make any difference to me whether you live in Speedsville or any other place, for I shall not be there for some time to come & I hope still to have the pleasure of corresponding with you as before. We are at Beltsville. I presume we shall go into winter quarters here, but it is rumored this morning that we are going to Harpers Ferry but I presume there is nothing in it because we are not in a very good condition to march. There is about 200 on the sick list. They are not all in the hospital but there is about 70 there and the rest are not able to do duty. Our camp can muster more than most any other company in the Regt and we cannot muster but 70 that are able to fight. On battalion drill the other day we only had 212 men from five companies which made only about 42 to a company. Our company had sixty-eight men. Lewis Strong is going to have his discharge in the course of two weeks. He has not ben able to work in five or six weeks. Lyman [James L.] Rightmier takes his place as orderly sergeant. He makes a first rate one. Two companies of the Regt are stationed between here and Washington. One company is within four miles. We are situated in a very pleasant place by the side of a peice of woods on a slight

The 109th had been in the service seven weeks. Many still did not have blankets or proper shoes. They often had to buy their own food. The health of the whole regiment was in peril. Amos Johnson wrote to his cousin Mary on October 22, 1862: "I wish that I could say that I was enjoying good health but I cannot, nor do I think that I ever shall if I stay a great while longer, for a person might about as well lie down and die as to try to get the doctors to do anything for him. There has been three of our regiment died this week in the hospital with the measles."

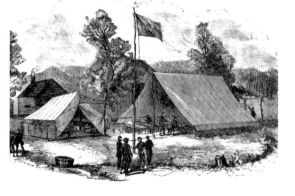

"Field hospital," Joseph W. Morton, Jr., Editor. *Sparks from the Camp Fire* (Philadelphia: Keystone Publishing Co., 1895) 109.

elevation of ground descending to the east. The weather continues to be pleasant and warm during the daytime but nights are very cold. I am in hopes we will go into winter quarters before long if not here, somewhere else. I wish McClellan would push on to Richmond as fast as possible so as to end this war. If we have to go into winter quarters before Richmond is in our possession and thereby have to lay inactive during the winter months, it seems to me as if it would be impossible to ever subdue them. I have made up my mind that the war will end within one year from the time I enlisted. It does not look much like it now I must confess, but stranger things have happened. We had a skirmish drill last Wednesday for the first time. We went two miles, loading and firing. We loaded with blank cartridges. Sometimes we loaded & fired standing up, and sometimes laying down. It is downright fun to practice skirmish drills. We do not have to drill very hard now & do not have to be on guard but once in eight days and then we have the whole company on to once. I got the box of things you & other kind friends from Speedsville sent me. I cannot express my heart felt thanks for the many good things that I have received. I will ever remember them & I hope I may someday be able to repay them. The mittens for the ears that you sent me comes first rate these cold nights. It did not rain here any last Sunday; it was quite a pleasant day. I tell you what we did, we did have quite a march. I guess you would have thought so if you had of seen us when we arrived here. We have not got a new colonel yet. Tracy is still Colonel but is acting as Brigadier General of this railroad. He has command of the road from Baltimore to Washington. Lieutenant Colonel Catlin got married yesterday to a very pretty girl from Owego. Give my best respects to your sister and tell her I hope she gets well soon. Mat sends his best regards. Hoping to hear from you soon, I remain as ever your friend,

John

Like John, many in the Union Army thought the capture of Richmond, the Confederate Capital, was the key to a quick victory and end to the war. General George B. McClellan, sometimes referred to as "The Young Napoleon," was eager to amass a huge, consolidated, well-drilled and disciplined army in order to inflict a massive blow against the rebellion and to capture Richmond. While an able administrator and skillful tactician, McClellan proved agonizingly reluctant to commit his superior numbers to the test. See, for example, David G. Martin. *The Peninsula Campaign March-July 1862* (Conshohocken, PA: Combined Books, 1992) 7-26.

Permission to reproduce this letter granted by the late Marian Gallagher and the Gallagher family. Letter transcribed by Marian Gallagher.

Savage Station. Nov. 23, 1862

Friend Amelia,

It is with pleasure that I seat myself this pleasant afternoon to impart to you a few thoughts that wander through my mind. They may not be very interesting to you but as my friend I hope you will except this letter and think I intended to make it interesting if it is not! Your letter was duly received and perused with more pleasure than you can imagine. I was very sorry indeed to hear that you had got so disagreable a comforter as a felon but we are all afflicted one way or annother and always will be as long as the wourld stands. I think you have done first rate writing with your teeth for the first time, better than I could do. Well I suppose you want to know the news about whether we go to Texas or not. I am very happy to inform you that we are not. We left Beltsville last Thursday morning & arrived here at two in the afternoon, a distance of ten miles. It commenced to rain shortly after we started and rained all day and night. It rained as hard as it could pore down. We was a pretty looking lot of soldiers you had better beleive. We put up our tents on the cold wet ground and sleept with nothing under us but an oil cloth blanket, which very soon wet through and being pretty wet you must calculate we sleept good! We are now encamped on our old camping ground. It seems quite like home again

Soldiers drilling, location and date unknown. Mathew Brady. Collection of Tioga County Historical Society. John Tidd wrote to Amelia that "it is downright fun to practice skirmish drills."

A "felon" is a painful infection, usually formed near the nail of a finger, thumb, or toe. As result of this infection Amelia lost the first joint of her thumb.

to get back to our home, as the boys call it. We are going into winter quarters here. Our Company is going to be sepperate from the rest of the Regt. Two Companys are stationed at the Junction, two at Beltsville, two between Beltsville and Bladensburg, and three at Laurel, the headquarters of the 109th. The 141th has got to go to Washington. I dont beleive that I can come home this winter. They have got through giveing furloughs, but you dont care do you whether I come or not. I presume you would not care about seeing my unworthy self! Burnside is pushing onward to Richmond as fast as posible. I am in hopes he will do better than McClellan has done but no one can tell. But of one thing I am certain. That is, if the war dont end by the first of next May we might as well acknowledge the Southern Confederacy for if we cannot whip them by that time, we never can! I will send you a likeness of McClellan so you can remember him when peace is once more in the land. George Parker is now in Philadelphia in the hospital. He is not very sick but not

The Confederacy reached its high water mark of success in the fall of 1862. Great Britain was on the verge of recognizing the Confederate States of America as a legitimate country. Catton, *Short History*, 94. However, by the end of the year, the Union was going back on the offensive; then, General Ambrose E. Burnside's Army took a beating at Fredericksburg on December 13, 1862.

General Ambrose E. Burnside, left, and General George B. McClellan, right. Collection of Michael Colella.

able to do duty. The soldiers like the change very well as far as I know. A change in Generals I mean. I dont think there is any danger of your being under the Southern rule for as you say, they would get a hard customer! I presume they would be glad to get rid of you, but you are not half so bad as you would have folks beleive. I have seen worse at least. There is a vacancy in the Lint Department; I beleive I will use my influence for you. If I accomplish the work I will let you know in my next. Mat [Parker] has ben promoted to Eighth Corporal. He and I are great friends. I did not see Old Abe or Seward. I was going to take dinner with Uncle Abe but had not time. I have lost my knife that I had when I left home. I lost it when we first came to the Junction, but have got annother one, but not near as good. I dont get as many letters from Speedsville as I did. You beat them all in writing so far & hope you will continue to do so. Oh dear, how I would like to go home. It seems as

John's morale seems to slip when he realizes the war probably will be a long one and that he is not likely to see "action" for months, if at all. He expresses regret that he is not receiving the volume of mail from home that he once did. He alludes to the possibility of being bored in winter quarters. John jokes about using his influence to get Amelia a job in the "Lint Department." To stanch bleeding and to provide dressings to wipe pus and other secretions, some women shredded linen, producing lint. Neither they nor the medical profession knew that this practice was unsanitary and in fact could cause infections.

Photograph of President Lincoln by Mathew Brady. Collection of Tioga County Historical Society.

though it had ben an age since I left Speedsville but it has not ben but a little over three months! We will have easy times here this winter. Nothing to do but to be up three hours every other night. Well, I cannot think of any more to write at presant. Give my respects to your sister. Write soon and excuse poor writing. So good bye Amelia. Your friend,

John Tidd.

Direct to Beltsville for the presant.

This following letter fragment on page 49 presumably continues from a letter previously begun, but not finished. The first part of the letter has not been located. Courtesy of Berkshire Historian's Office.

December 5, 1862

… I will now try and finish this letter. We was ordered to guard all the crossroads about here and also double the guard on the railroad for the purpose of preventing persons from running away from the draft that took place here in this county day before yestarday. I went out with four men at eight oclock and staid till half past twelve. We was then releived. We did not arrest anyone but a negro. We marched him ten or fifteen rods just for the fun of it and then let him go. He was somewhat frightened and promised he would

not be out after nine oclock after this. Well I must tell you about the dinner we had the other day. The folks from Berkshire, Newark and West Newark sent this company a Thanksgiving dinner. They sent four large boxes full of every thing you could think of. They did not get here in time for Thanksgiving so we had it last Sunday. The Col, Quartermaster and Dr. [S. B.] Hunt ate dinner with us. We set the table here in the grove. It was large enough for the whole company to sit down at once. We had chicken pie,

Despite John's endorsement of President Lincoln's Emancipation Proclamation (letter of September 26) and the North's elevation of anti-slavery as an issue and as a claim for the moral high ground in waging the war, many Northerners were apathetic toward the institution of slavery and some remained downright hostile toward the notion of slave liberation. John, in this letter, betrays his willingness to see the freed slave as a simple buffoon to fool, tease, and laugh at. In an earlier letter (September 14), he referred casually to "niggers" as somehow less than human. For Southern and Northern attitudes and prejudices toward blacks and the institution of slavery, see for example, Peter Batty and Peter Perish. *The Divided Union: The Story of the Great American War, 1861-65* (Topsfield, MA: Salem House Publishers, 1987) 10-41. Photograph of Union soldiers, including a black man, by Mathew Brady. Collection of Tioga County Historical Society.

roast turkeys, five kinds of cake, two kinds of pie, butter, cheese, bread, coffee and other things too numerous to mention. I think the boys done justice to the eatibles; I did for one at least. I think I never eat so much before in my life. I am shure I never eat any thing that tasted so good before in my life. The men are all bringing their wives down here this winter. I dont know but I shall have to send for mine. What do you say? I will try and see Abe before I come back, and all the other big guns & chiefs. I dont know why they divided the regiment unless it is to guard a longer distance of the railroad. As far as being together is concerned, we had rather be alone by ourselves. The helth of the regiment is pretty good at present. Full as good I think as it would be up North. Miss Stratton is going to teach writing school in Speedsville again this winter I understand. I wish I could go. I think you write pretty well for one that is so sadly afflicted. I can read your letters easy enough. I presume, full as easy as you can read mine. I have'nt heard anything from Elson since he left Owego, only that he was seen in Elmira the day he left Owego. I think he was foolish to run away after he had enlisted. I wonder where he has gone.

I remain your friend,

John

Sarah A. Palmer, also known as "Aunt Becky," left her Ithaca, New York, home and two daughters in early September 1862 to serve as a nurse for the Union wounded and sick. Sarah Palmer and the hospital cooks at Beltsville, Maryland, proposed to have a Thanksgiving dinner for the hospital patients and other guests, 118 people in all. Unable to obtain the required food, permission was granted to go out in the country to see what they could find. "They returned with wild and tame turkeys, and pigs, and chickens and we were soon on the high road to success. Our pies Coleman and I made at night, and I cut out two hundred biscuit, thinking bread would eke out the supply, but we must have some of our home fixings, or it would not seem like Thanksgiving." S. A. Palmer. *The Story of Aunt Becky's Army-Life* (New York: John F. Trow & Co., 1867 and reprinted in 1996 by Talbothays Books, Aurora, New York) 12-13.

Timothy H. O'Sullivan, 1863. Noncommissioned officers' mess of Co. D, 93rd New York Infantry. Library of Congress, Prints and Photographs.

Savage Station. December 19th / 1862

Friend Amelia,

It is with pleasure that I once more seat myself for the purpose of answering your kind and welcome letter which was received last evening. It is a great privlage to write and receive letters from those whom we know to be true friends. It does not satisfy the mind to converse with the pen as much as it would by the word of mouth, but still it is a sorce of great enjoyment, especialy to those who are far from home and friends and all the privliges & enjoyments that they have ben in the habit of enjoying while at home. No one knows anything about a soldiers life till they have tried its realty's. We here in this Regt know but a little of the hardships and privations to what some of our soldiers do that have ben in the service for a year and ahalf, but I think there is a good chance for us to see and experiance all the hardships that have ben gone through by those that have ben longer in the service if this war goes on. It looks rather dark at presant. Burnside has ben defeated and forced to recross the Rappahannock.

With the tumultuous events of the Civil War's 1862 autumn season behind them—Pope's defeat at the Second Battle of Bull Run, the prospect of Lee's invasion of Washington, "Stonewall" Jackson's success at Harper's Ferry, McClellan's fight to a draw (at best) against Lee at Antietam, Burnside's disastrous rout by Lee's Confederates at Fredericksburg—the situation looked bad, but poor weather allowed both sides to regroup, rest, and dig in for the winter.

View of Fredericksburg, Virginia, from east bank of the Rappahannock. Timothy H. O'Sullivan, 1863. Library of Congress, Prints and Photographs.

I think the rebels will never be whiped unless the President carry's his Proclamation into effect and I dont know as they can be then, but I am satisfied that they never can without. We have got our barracks all made and have moved into them. They are made of pine logs, nine feet wide and fourteen feet long. They are six feet high & are covered with our cloth tents. There are eight men in each one. We have a stove for each barrack. They are warm and comfortable, much better than any I have seen any soldiers have since we have ben here. I dont know as we will stay here all winter, but I presume we will for the inhabitants about here wrote the congressman of these countys. I understand they have sent in a petition to the war department to let this Regt guard this railroad as long as it has to be guarded. It is the best behaved regiment that ever was on this road. It is all owing to its officers. The colonel and

"Culinary department." Johnson, Ridpath, and others. *Campfire and Battlefield,* 44.

our captain both make the men behave themselves as well as they would to home and some of them a good deal better. They are not alowed to drink a drop of anything that will intoxicate or use any disrespectful language to the citizzens. If they do, they are put on double duty for a week. The 141th N.Y.V. that were stationed here stole everything they could lay their hands on. They were sent away. My throat has got well and I hope your thumb has got along as well. We have ben in the service four months and ahalf and hav'nt received any pay yet, only what we got at Binghamton. We are mustered for pay once in two months. It soon will be time to muster the second time since we have ben here in Maryland. Although we muster for pay, we dont always get it. You must'nt feel so bad about my taking a sleigh ride with Hellen [Amelia's sister] this winter. I dont beleive I shall be home to take a ride with anyone very soon. When I do, if that time ever comes. I will, if you wish, take the pleasure of riding with you before I do anyone else. I will not ever except Hellen. I dont expect to come home until this war is closed, which will not be very soon by the way the war is carried on now. Well, I cannot think of anymore to write now. Please write soon. Good night & pleasant dreams.

From your true and sincere friend,

John

Company B had missed all the battles and increasingly became part of "The Railroad Regiment," charged with the unglamorous and seemingly never ending task of guarding the Baltimore and Ohio between Baltimore and Washington, as well as the telegraph lines. The men's primary work turned to ensuring their comfort as best they could and to prepare for the tedium of inactivity. There did not appear to be any prospects of getting into the fight, which many joined to do and which many increasingly desired.

Going to Try Like Thunder

In the darkness he saw visions of a thousand-tongued fear that would babble at his back and cause him to flee, while others were going coolly about their country's business. He admitted that he would not be able to cope with this monster. He felt that every nerve in his body would be an ear to hear the voices, while other men would remain stolid and deaf.

—Stephen Crane, *The Red Badge of Courage*, 1895

With the conclusion of the Battle of Fredericksburg, Union and Confederate Armies began to settle in for the winter. Both sides were aware that living conditions would be harsh, with snow, rain, winds, and cold making their summer tents and warm weather living arrangements unsuitable. Charles Carleton Coffin witnessed preparations for the winter of 1863: "It was surprising to see how quickly the soldiers made themselves comfortable in huts chinked with mud and roofed with split shingles. These rude dwellings had a fireplace at one end, doors hung on leathern hinges, and bunks one above another, like berths in a steamboat. There the men told stories, played checkers and cards, read the newspapers, wrote letters to their friends far away, and kept close watch all the while upon the enemy. … But there were dark days and dreary nights. It tried their endurance and patriotism to stand all night upon picket, with the north wind howling around them and the snow whirling into drifts. There were rainy days, and weeks of mud, when there was no drilling, and when there was nothing to do."

For the men of the 109th, this period was distasteful. Their winter quarters were cramped. A typical 9-by-14-foot shelter for five to seven soldiers was dirty and poorly ventilated, despite the cold drafts that always found entrance somewhere. Late autumn weather continued with heavy rains and cold winds.

Johnson, Ridpath, and others. *Campfire and Battlefield,* cover.

Then snow came off and on through February. The soldiers' heavy wool coats eventually became soggy and never seemed to dry properly. Conditions ground the men down. Constant exposure to the elements, lack of proper food, and poor living conditions were fertile breeding grounds for sickness. Scarlet fever became prevalent in the 109th. Those afflicted were sent to Mason's Island, near Washington, in an effort to stop the dread disease's spread. To top things off, soldiers in the 109th usually didn't receive their pay on time and often were owed as much as four months' wages.

Uncomfortable as conditions were, the men tried to cheer themselves with gossip, games, gambling, and music. Some defied regulations and yielded to the lure of strong spirits and inevitable drunkenness. Some sought the comforts of loose women. But despite their best efforts, the soldiers guarding the railroad, bridges, and telegraph lines were bored, lonesome, and homesick. Morale was low. And nagging at the back of their minds were the dismal failures and ineptitudes of Union forces in recent battles, foremost of which were their defeat in

Charles Carleton Coffin. *The Boys of '61* (Boston: Estes and Lauriat, 1896) 215.

Burying the Federal dead, Fredericksburg, Virginia. Timothy H. O'Sullivan, 1864. Collection of Tioga County Historical Society.

mid-December at the Battle of Fredericksburg and the draw at the Battle of Stones River ("Murfreesboro"), in Tennessee, in the waning days of December 1862 and the first days of 1863. Union troops had failed to advance farther upon the vital rail center of Chattanooga. Many felt that Johnny Reb could never be beaten. Still, many wanted to get into the fight.

At the end of two years' fighting, nearly 200,000 soldiers from both sides had died and neither side was closer to securing what it had gone to war to gain. If someone insisted on selecting a winner at that time, however, the Confederate States of America might have been nominated. C.S.A. forces under General Lee had repulsed Union efforts to take their capital and seemed invincible in Virginia. Federal generals seemed timid, sluggish, petty, or plain incompetent. The war news of 1862 undermined morale among Union soldiers and left segments of the civilian population depressed and fearful for the preservation of the United States. Historian James McPherson noted that the nation almost did not survive the events of 1862 and the first half of 1863.

But matters were to improve dramatically in the latter part of 1863. President Lincoln replaced General Ambrose E. Burnside with General Joseph ("Fighting Joe") Hooker as Commander of the Army of the Potomac on January 25, an inevitable move after the disastrous performance of the former at Fredericksburg. General Hooker's men were defeated by General Lee's much smaller force in the Battle of Chancellorsville in early May. In late June, after continuing spats with President Lincoln and Lincoln's advisor and chief of staff, Henry W. Halleck, Hooker yielded command to General George Gordon Meade. Meade immediately made desperate preparations to stop Lee's advance into Pennsylvania. Meade's diligence paid dividends in the early July Battle of Gettysburg, when the Union troops forced Lee's severely diminished army back into Virginia.

Major General Ulysses S. Grant, appointed Commander of

all forces in the west on January 29, 1863, began the Vicksburg Campaign to open the Mississippi River to the Union. Grant began winning battle after battle in Mississippi. He also replaced lethargic General William S. Rosecrans with General George H. "Pap" Thomas in Chattanooga.

The Congressional Conscription Act of March 3, 1863, required Northern males aged 20 to 45 to enroll in the draft. This legislation was unpopular, and draft riots in New York City resulted in widespread death and property destruction.

Confederate dead gathered for burial, Gettysburg, Pennsylvania. Alexander Gardener, 1863. Library of Congress, Prints and Photographs.

The war's scorecard of 1863 from the Union's perspective could be tallied as follows. Battles won: Port Gibson, Jackson, Champion's Hill, Big Black River, and Vicksburg, Mississippi; Gettysburg, Pennsylvania; and Chickamauga, Georgia; Chattanooga, Lookout Mountain and Missionary Ridge, Tennessee. Battles lost: Chancellorsville, Virginia. Battles fought to a draw: Stones River ("Murfreesboro"), Tennessee; Brandy Station, Virginia; Charleston, South Carolina.

By year's end, the South was divided into two vertical parts geographically. The Union army was in northern Georgia, poised to launch an attack against Atlanta in the spring. Union military leaders cast their eyes southward once again, dreaming of capturing Richmond and other Confederate strongholds.

President Lincoln delivered his famous "Gettysburg Address" on November 19. The President also issued a Proclamation of Amnesty and Reconstruction on December 8, offering a pardon and amnesty to people engaged in the rebellion (other than high-ranking Confederacy government officials and military officers) if they would take an oath of allegiance to the United States, its laws, and its proclamations concerning slavery. Any Confederate state that produced allegiance oaths totaling at least 10 percent of citizens who had voted in 1860 could form a new state government recognized by the President. Congress would decide whether or not to seat Senators and Representatives elected by those newly-formed state entities. Thus, the olive branch was extended.

Savage. Switch. January 1st 1863

Friend. Amelia.

It is Newyears,
and it is cold & windy, another
year has past, and gone, and I am
afraid that with it, the end of
the best Government, that ever
the sun shone upon? What another
year, will bring forth God. only kn
ows, but it seems to me as if we
never could conquer the Southerns
to tell the truth, about it, since
the battle of Fredericksburg. I have
given up all hopes of whiping
them. I dont know as I should so
express myself, for I would like

Savage Switch. January 1st, 1863

Friend Amelia,

It is Newyear's and it is cold & windy. Annother year has past and gone and I am afraid that with it the end of the best Government that ever the sun shone upon! What annother year will bring forth, God only knows, but it seems to me as if we never could conquer the Southerners. To tell the truth about it, since the Battle of Fredericksburg, I have given up all hopes of whiping them. I dont know as I should so express myself, for I would like to see the union troops victorious and the union of these states preserved as much as any other person, but still I cannot help my thoughts. I am not alone in this. Pretty much every soldier in this Regt & also other Regiments think the same as myself. I received your much wished for answer to my last letter Tuesday evening last and have taken this opportunity to answer it. This is the only privledge that I have got this Happy New Years, as some call it, but to me it is not a very happy day. I was up all night last night, and to day I am sitting by a poor fire by the side of a railroad bridge where I have got to remain till six oclock this evening a writing to one who is many miles away, but who is as dear to me as she could be if she were daly within the sound of my voice. You must not be offended at what I say for I am lawless like all other soldiers. Mat is as well as usual again. It is very helthy here this winter. There has ben only one death in our company as yet. We were muster'd for pay yesterday which makes four months pay they owe us for now. The Colonel praised us very highly. He said we were the best looking company in the Regt. Dont you think it quite a compliment? The 137th are at Fairfax Corthouse. I suppose they had the pleasure of shooting at a few rebels there last week by the reports. I have not heard much from Speedsville for the last two or three weeks. I understand it is quite sickly there. I forgot to tell you that one of our men had deserted

On January 1, 1863, 70,219 staff, infantry, cavalry, and artillery were defending Washington, an increase of 8,181 from December 1862. The 109th was headquartered at Annapolis Junction, Maryland, and later at Falls Church, Virginia. Ten companies were spread between Annapolis Junction and Washington; five at Falls Church; three at Mason's Island, Maryland, one in Laurel, Maryland, and one in Bladensburg, Maryland.

and gone home. He staid all night to Mr. Reeds the night before we went to Binghamton. His name is Amzi Mead the fellow that swore so. You wanted to know about them photographs. I have asked for some of the girls pictures but they dont feel inclined to send them as yet. I know how to obey orders but I dont like to in this case. But if you dont think enough

Collapsible writing board with ink and pen. Collection of Michael Colella.

of me to let me keep it even if I don't get any from the other girls, why I suppose I shall have to comply with your demand. George Haynes gets along finely. He stands it without anything to drink much better than I expected. He has not drinked but a very little since we have ben in Maryland. The officers cannot get licquor much easir than privates. I had to stay in camp all day Chrismas day and was so unfortnate as to not get a single thing as a presant on that day. They did not use me as well as last year. I shall have to answer your questions as to whether I will ever give up fighting the rebels or not, by telling you that I never will desert till I am obliged to, which I hope will never be! Well, I must close. I cannot think of anything very interesting to write this time so you will have to put up with what I have wrote. Hoping to hear from you soon.

I remain your friend,

John
Annapolis Junction, M.D.

Savage Switch. January 10th, 1863

Friend Amelia,

   As the shades of another evening closes around our quiet
camp, I again seat myself, with pen in hand, to answer a letter
which I have just had the pleasure of receiving from your
own dear self. I am well as usual and hope these few lines will
find you enjoying the same blessing. Then you think I had
the blues when I wrote before, do you? Well, I did and have
got them still and dont know but what I shall continue to
have them unless you write often your Patriotic letters full of
encouragement and good advice. I suppose I had ought to be
more patriotic and more contented with a soldiers life than I
be, but it looks so discourageing that it is hard to beleive that
we will ever be able to conquor the Rebels. They are better
of to day than one year ago, have a larger force, and better
armed, and are more confident of success than ever before;

Recruiting office in New
York's City Hall Park.
Johnson, Ridpath, and
others. *Campfire and
Battlefield*, 286.

while our force, though largely increased since last year at this time, yet it is fast falling down to its old maximum number of last fall. Before the last call of six hundred thousand, a soldier writing from the Army of the Potomac, says that three fifth's of the whole force that has been raised since the war commenced are gone. Some killed, some deserted and a great many more of them have eather died in the hospitals with sickness or are now in the hospitals sick. He also says that McClellan's Army will not averge three hundred men to a Regt, and the new levies which includes our troops, will not averge much more than that. They say the 137th Regt will not muster three hundred for pay and they had as many men as we did. The two year men's time will be out next May & the nine month men. The army will then be so small that they will have to draft to fill the ranks again. But then, it is no matter about the soldiers. It dont make any differance whether they are all killed or not. They are not of any account. We are liveing about as usual, nothing to do but guard a little, but we have now got a job of building a fort near a railroad bridge here by the station. The weather is warm and pleasant the most of the time. George Haynes has resigned his commission and is going home. He has just returned from Washington where he has ben to get his pay. He got his resignation papers excepted and returned back to him within two days from the time he resigned. They were excepted by the recimendation of the Colonel. Mead did not have any reason for deserting as I know of but to go home and see his folks & to get out of the Army. The last heard of him, he was on his way to Canada. There has ben eight or ten deserted from this Regt. I would not desert if I knew we were going into battle to morrow. In fact, I am tired of staying around here. Would just as live go into the field as not, if I have got to, when it comes warm weather. It would be most to cold to sleep on the ground this winter. The negroes, I dont think I think any more of than you do, if I do as much.

John's prejudice against blacks was shared by many whites in his day. Most Federal soldiers were not concerned with freeing the slaves. President Lincoln's Administration had not emphasized that goal from the outset, although the Emancipation Proclamation added that as an objective. Historian Bruce Catton noted, "The average Federal soldier began his term of service either quite willing to tolerate slavery in the South or definitely in sympathy with it. He was fighting for the Union and for nothing more." Catton, *Short History*, 174. A little-noted provision of the Emancipation Proclamation, which went into effect on January 1, 1863, allowed blacks to serve in the Army and Navy. Frederick Douglass, an abolitionist orator and writer, was busy recruiting black soldiers for the famous Massachusetts 54th Volunteers to fight in the Civil War in segregated units under white officers. Men of the 54th made a doomed assault on Fort Wagner, South Carolina on July 18, 1863, during the Siege of Charleston. Often, black soldiers were put to work doing the routine dirty fatigue and grunt work of soldiering,

They are better off to day than we soldiers are and the poor whites also and it is all on account of slavery. But, it is to late now. I dont know as the freeing of the negroes will have any effect upon the rebellion, but it will not do any hurt. Elson has got home. He has ben to work in Canton, Bradford Co, Pennsylvania, near where my sister lives. He is home on a visit, is going back soon. Mr. Reed had a good party New Years. There was about sixty couples. Leon Blanchard waited on Mary. Dell Legg, dont you think he has come down a little? I went to Baltimore last week and saw the shipping. It was the nicest sight I have seen since I have ben here. Well, I think I have wrote enough for this time. More than you want to read I presume. Give my respects to your sister and write soon.

From your true and sincere friend.

John Tidd

but generally acquitted themselves creditably when pressed into battle. Catton, *Short History*, 177. Some 180,000 black men served in the army and another 30,000 saw duty in the navy before the war ended, with some 68,000 killed or wounded.

"Storming Fort Wagner," Massachusetts 54th Volunteers, Kurz & Allison, 1890, Library of Congress, Prints and Photographs.

Savage Switch, M.D., Feb 20th, 1863

Friend Amelia,

I received your most welcome letter last evening, and
being somewhat tired, having been to Washington, I
postponed writing till this morning. I was very sorry indeed
to hear of your sisters death. It is hard to loose a sister. I know
it would be hard for me to loose one and perhaps it is harder
for you than it would be for me. I dont know as I can find
anything that will be very interesting to write to you about,
but I will do the best I can. We have not gone to Washington
yet as you suppose and I guess we will not go. They have got
annother Regt there where we were going. Some think we
will stay here all next summer but I cannot hardly beleive it.
We have been here now longer than any other Regt. April
or May I think will see us crossing the Potomac. Day before

Patent Office, Washington.
Mathew Brady. Collection
of Tioga County Historical
Society.

yestarday the snow fell ten inches deep and this morning it is
pleasant and not a bit of snow to be seen. Snow dont stay on
long here. We are captureing a good many paroled prisoners
here now, deserters from Annapolis City. They go through
here in squad's from two to twenty five. We have had three
desertions from our company. Other companys have suffered
worse. James L. Rightmire is Secont Lieut. There has been
quite a change in the non-commissioned officers since we
were to Binghamton. I will send you a list of the Sergeants
& Corporals & Privates. There is one promotion yet to be
made. I will write as it is now. I went to Washington as I said,
yestarday. Went into the Patent Office. There is everything
you can think of in there. Washington's cloes & camp

The U.S. Capitol, Wash-
ington. Mathew Brady.
Collection of Tioga County
Historical Society.

equipment, his tent that he tented in, sword & portfolio. Infact, you can see everything that was ever made. There is a great many wounded soldiers there. I tell you, it looks hard to see them wounded in the feet, arms and most every place you can think of. I also went to the Capitol and in Congress. They were debating about giving the President so much power they will make a king of him yet. He is pretty near that now. They are trying to pass a bill to give the President the whole power—due away with the Supreme Court & taking away the rights of the governor's of a state, to call out the troops on a draft or any other way. A man now, if he can raise three hundred dollars, can get rid of going to war. But, if he cannot raise it he has got to go. What justice is there in such a law as that? None at all, a law for the rich! There will soon be a draft. Then we will have plenty of company in misery. I think it will set some of the Speedsville boys to thinking when they call a draft of about seventy thousand from New York State, dont you? I wish you could come down here and go through the Capitol & Patent Office. It would be a great treat. No, I dont think McClellan is guilty of any neglect & neather do I beleive he could be found guilty if he should have his trial. I did not get any Valentines but if there had been any good one's here I presume you would have received one, but never mind, there are better day's comeing. It is now over six months since I left home. It seems a good while and if you want to get back to Speedsville as bad as I do, you want to get back pretty bad. I am not exactly homesick but had rather live in Old Speedsville. There is quite a good many cases of fever now in the hospital. Frank Taylor is in the hospital; has been in there about two weeks. Well, I cannot think of any more to write at present. I guess it will be hard work to read this. Write soon. Your friend,

John Tidd

Legislation providing for inducting men into the military, about to be enacted by the U.S. Congress in early March, 1863, was necessary due to serious military manpower losses through enlistment expirations. John's resentment toward men in Speedsville who did not volunteer, his hope they would be conscripted, his disdain for the ability of some draftees to pay a commutation fee of $300 for an exemption (nearly a year's wages for an unskilled worker), his contempt for deserters, his horror at seeing war casualties, and his increasing feelings of being abandoned by those back home make this and the next letter profound expressions of cynicism and discouragement.

General McClellan had major enemies among politicians. Some spread rumors that he was sympathetic to the Confederacy and was quietly stalling and failing when he did lead Union forces in battle so as to assist the South in winning the war. In short, at the highest level, these hostile and virulent voices were accusing him of being a

Savage Switch, M.D. March 12th, 1863

Friend Amelia,

I received your most welcome letter last night and have
with much pleasure availed myself of this early opportunity
to respond to it. It is a very warm and pleasant day indeed.
It seems more like summer than winter but it is about time
for warm weather down here. It is still very windy. The boys
are pretty helthy in this company. We have not had but one
man in the hospital now for a good while till yestarday. There
were two taken there. Frank Taylor is a little better. You want
to know if I think I can get a furlough this spring. No, I dont
beleive I can or anyone else in this Regt. Furloughs has played
out. I am afraid Congress has passed a law to give furloughs
but the President has all the power & things go just as he
says. But if there is any furloughs given, I think I can get one.
I dont like to own that I am a Democrat but dont know but
I shall have to. I think I am just as good a Democrat now as
yourself, but no Secession Democrat. I remember Hooker
Deland. I think there is no dought but what he knows the
government's plans better than the Cabinet, especily if he is
as smart as Charlie. By the way, how does he stand on the
war question now? Does he think he will stand a draft? Then
you think you will not stand a draft, do you. Now you need
not think you can get out of it in that way. If you do, I will
have Captain Hyde detail me to go and force you, the same
as they are trying to do to Hub Reed. Then I guess you will
come willingly for I think I should be more successful than
the Captain was. I would take you by surprise! I hope they
take Hub Reed. He was so fierce for going & getting other
folks to enlist over to Berkshire & then to back out. It was
mean. We dont have any thing to do now but we have had
it pretty hard since we have been here. When we first came
here we had to be up most every night and drill during the
day & for two weeks our company were up every night. That

traitor. That this was never
seriously accepted by the
public was demonstrated
by the fact that McClellan
became the Democrat's
candidate in the national
election of 1864 and won
nearly 45 percent of the
popular vote. During his
candidacy, he did not
repudiate the war, although
he was critical of the way it
had been managed. Catton,
Short History, 212, 229.

is two hours on & four of. While down to Beltsville, we went two miles and drilled four hours every afternoon & drilled on company drill in the forenoon. But, that is nothing to what we will have to come to, I presume. I don't know what made [George L.] Haynes resign, but presume because he got tired of military life. Yes, we have got quite a number of women here but they are no company for me. There is not one of them I am acquainted with. Besides, we are not allowed to run around much. If there were fifty sick ones in the company, they would not be any better cared for on account of the women being here. As soon as one is sick, they are sent to the hospital, there they are waited on by men. Write soon with all the news.

Ever Yours,

John

Early in the war, male medical officers resented the strong-willed women who were assigned as nurses, surgeon's assistants, or even as surgeons, and did what they could to drive the women away. Eventually, however, women in hospitals came to be appreciated, especially by the recuperating or dying soldiers. Elizabeth D. Leonard, "Mary Walker, May Surratt, and Some Thoughts on Gender in the Civil War" in Catherine Clinton and Nina Silber, editors. *Battle Scars: Gender and Sexuality in the American Civil War* (New York: Oxford University Press, 2006) 104-119.

Nurses and officers of the U.S. Sanitary Commission, Fredericksburg, Virginia. James Gardner, 1864. Library of Congress, Prints and Photographs.

Savage Switch. April 8th, 1863

Dear Friend,

As the shades of annother evening settle down upon the
earth and all nature sinks to repose, my thoughts wander
back to the many, many happy hours that I have spent in
your company and to the time before we parted, and it may
be, parted forever. May the Lord grant me the privalige of
living through this trying ordeal and return once more to the
many dear friends and relations that I have left behind. Oh,
how long it seems since I had the pleasure of seeing you last,
almost an age, but I dare say, it seems nearly as long to you as
it does to me. Eight long months have passed and gone and
still the war is not ended, but the prospect is getting brighter.
The day is breaking. The southerners begin to tremble in their
shoes at the mighty power of the Government. The union
army is very strong and is gaining strength every day. Two or
three regiments of deserters come back every week under the
President's procklimation. A [Amzi] Mead has come back to
this company. He came the first day of April. He was glad
enough to get back. The news from Charleston to day looks
good. It is reported that it was attacked last Thursday and
taken. If it proves true, the rebels are gone up and that before
long to. The soldiers are getting greatly encouraged. Things
look brighter then for a long time before and I think it is
about time that something was done. We have played long
enough with the traitors. They must now surrender or die!
I dont know how long we will stay here. No one can tell. I
should not be surprised if we did not leave here this summer,
but I dont know much more about it than you do. I was
surprised that you left Speedsville. I had not got a letter from
you in so long a time that I had almost begun to think you
had forgotten me entirely, but that idea was erased from my
mind tonight when I received the ever welcome letter. Now
you see I am answering right away. Now see if you cannot do

In fact, Fort Sumter's cannons, guarding Charleston,
sank Union Admiral
Samuel F. Du Pont's ship
the *Keokuk* and seriously
damaged other ironsides
in his fleet on April 7.
Later, when Rear Admiral
John A. Dahlgren arrived
in the harbor, Union ships
pounded Sumter into
rubble. Still, Charleston
held out against Federal
capture until early 1865.
Robert M. Ketchum, Edi-
tor. *The American Heritage
Picture History of The Civil
War* (New York: American
Heritage Publishing Co.,
Inc. 1960) 191.

the same by me. I have got an ambrotype that I had taken about six weeks ago when I was in Washington. It is very good but would have liked it better with my cap of. I am a little fleshier now than I was then. I weigh sixteen pounds more than when I enlisted. I would be very much pleased if you would get an ambrotype taken for me & send it to me. They look more lifelike. I will send the ambrotype. If you dont like it I will get a photograph and send it the first chance I get. You need not be afraid of my letting the rebels get our flag. I will stand by it till the last. It is now floating over the soil of Maryland on a pole most as high as the Speedsville pole. I am in hopes to help raise it in Speedsville once more. I had not heard that Hellen was going to Dryden till I got your letter. So you see, I dont learn everything that is going on there. Sergeant [Howard] M. Hubbard is very sick with the feaver & is not expected to live. I would liked to have been to the exhibition very much but could not come. I dont know as you can read this but if it bothers you to much burn it up. Give my respects to Theo, Nettie and Charlie please. I am acquainted with him.

From your affectionate friend,

John

John promised Amelia that he wouldn't let the Rebels capture the flag. "I will stand by it until the last." The Second Battle of Bull Run. Currier and Ives, c. 1862. Library of Congress, Prints and Photographs.

Ambrotypes were photographic negatives on glass. When laid on a black background, the appearance of a positive print was revealed. They were considered superior to their predecessor, the daguerreotype, because they did not produce a glare and they could be mounted so they were not a reverse image of the original. Robert Taft. *Photography and the American Scene: A Social History, 1839-1889* (New York: Dover Publications, Inc., 1964) 123-127.

Savage Switch. April 26, 1863

Dear Friend,

Annother Sabbath morning has dawned upon our most
unhappy country. It is a very pleasant day here in this
southern clime. I thought I would devote a few leisure
moments in addressing a few thoughts to one of my much
estemed friends, is no dought thinking of the absent soldiers
or soldier who often thinks and meditates on the past
pleasures of home, and who sometimes even thinks they are
enjoying the pleasures of the home circle. But these thoughts
are only felt in midnight dreams. One cannot realize what it
is to be a soldier till they have tryed its realtys. We dont know
much about soldiering to what some Regts do but we have
seen enough to judge about what it is. Hard as it is, we are all
willing to endure the hardships and privations of a soldier's
life. I to, leave home, friends and all the comforts with which

"The soldier's dream of
home." Currier & Ives,
1861-65. Library of
Congress, Prints and
Photographs.

we were surrounded and go forth and fight the enemys of
our Country. If it will only restore peace and harmony to
this now distracted country. If it will restore the union as it
was, I would willingly face the Rebels on the battlefield. I
will try and keep up good courage till the wicked rebellion is
brought to a successful isue. I feel as if I could fight the south
with as good courage now as ever. In fact, I have wished for
some time past that we would go in the front. I have got sick
staying here. It is so lonesome. I dont know how much longer
we will stay here. Some say we will not stay much longer, but
they dont anyone know anything about it.

I am glad you like it so well there & that there are so many
nice young gentlemen there. I hope you will not fall in love
with any of them for what would us boys from Speedsville
do if you should lose your heart. I am sure I would not live
through it, would not want to at least. Hubbard was taken
sick within two or three days after he got back. He was not
expected to live at one time but he is better now. They most
all come back sick. Six have been home from this company.
Joel Allen came back day before yesterday. Three go at a time
from each company. If they keep giveing furloughs, I think I
can get one about the first of July. The Proclimation that the
deserters come back on was one that he isued in February
last, offering them, if they would come back by the first day
of April, he would not punish them. He would only take
their pay away from them while they were gone. There were
as many as a Regiment a week that came back for the last few
days. Deserting is stoped now almost entirely. A man that will
desert now ought to be shot and will be. They are going to
make an example of the first two or three that desert from this
Regt. They will be shot without any doubt. The guard house
has also played out for all those that disobey the laws. They
have a court martial & are sentenced to work on public works
from five to sixty days. We have got one, Anson Partridge, I
think he will be sentenced for sixty days. He is now confined

Desertion of duty was
fairly common, particularly
after the Conscription Act
yielded substitute soldiers.
A drafted man could be
permanently exempt if
he provided a substitute,
leading to many sick, shift-
less, or dim-witted people
being put forward. Another
unfortunate outcome of
the act was the bounty-
jumper, who profited from
the cash incentives paid
by cities, townships, counties, districts, states, and
the federal government to
encourage volunteers rather
than have to resort to the
unpopular draft system.
The "volunteers" were often
slackers who would col-
lect the bounties and then
desert at the first opportunity, sometimes to repeat
the process in different
locales under false names.
The bounty collectors
who stayed in the service
often were next to useless
as soldiers. From time to
time, captured deserters
were executed to provide
an example to those who

in a fort waiting for trial. His offense is drunkenness. I dont know why I should not beleive you in earnest when you wished me to send my photograph. I certainly had as live you would have it as anyone, for I am sure I have no better friend. I dont think you want to be ancious in the least. I hope you think better of me than to think I would judge you so harshly. I hope you will keep the picture. You can have it with pleasure. I dont know as the girls need to be jelous because you have more pictures than they. They dont know as you have any, unless you have told them. If they dont like it they can do the other thing. I would be very happy to have you send me your Ambrotype. Send me that and I will send your photograph back. I like the Ambrotype best. We have had some very rainy weather here lately, raining most every day. For something to pass away the time, I borrow books from folks in Savage Village, about a mile from here. We had a grand review last Sunday at Laurel. I tell you they looked splendid. The ladies of the place were out to see us parade. You ought to see us on parade now. I think we make a better appearance than we did at Binghamton. Every man steps at once when we march. Write soon.

From your dearest friend,

John

might be tempted to steal away from their units. In the Union Army, 141 executions were documented. However, President Lincoln was sympathetic to many men who gave good reasons for desertion and granted many pardons. He preferred, he said, to "take the risk on the side of mercy." Ketchum, *American Heritage,* 381, 485. Also see John's April 26 letter.

Marching on parade was a favorite activity for soldiers far from the battlefields. "Pigtail" bugle. Collection of Michael Colella.

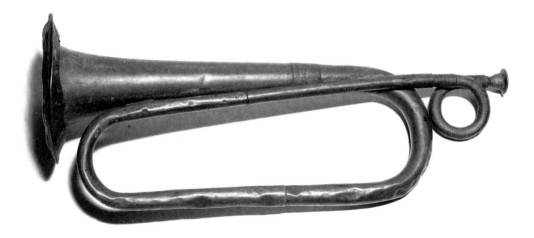

Savage Switch. May 14th, 1863

My Dear Friend,

It is with pleasure that I again have the opportunity to address a few words to you in answer to your most welcome letter that came to hand last evening. I am happy to inform you that we are still guarding the railroad with not much prospect of moving, but to tell you the truth about it, I am not very well pleased with the prospect for I am anxious to go and help put down this Rebellion, the greatest Rebellion the world ever saw & the most wicked. For two years Jeff & his minions have spread terror and desolation throughout the land, but I trust their career is about ended. I wish I could just go down and help Gen. Hooker take Richmond. If nothing more, it would be quite a treat to help take the Rebel Capitol. I think if they should take that it would end the

The Battle of Chancellorsville, Virginia, was a Union defeat and ended Hooker's bravado and legend as a fighter.

The Battle of Chancelorsville. Kurz & Allison, 1889. Library of Congress, Prints and Photographs.

war. It was rumored that it had been taken, but it was false. Gen Hooker did not do as well as it was expected of him but he was not defeated. He was forced to recross the river on account of the rain. I hope he will soon make annother advance on the Rebels. I was in Washington last Saturday. The streets were full of officers & soldiers. A great many Colonels & Captains & Privates were running around with their heads, arms and feet done up caused by wounds received in the late battles. While there, I had an opportunity of hearing what the soldiers thought of Gen Hooker & the war. They have great confidence in his abilities. I asked one if they got very badly whiped. He told me they did

General Hooker. Hand colored photograph by Mathew Brady. Collection of Tioga County Historical Society.

not get whipped. He said they killed two to one & whipped them every time. It is surprising to see what a difference of feeling there is now with regard to the war to what it was last winter. You cannot hardly find a soldier now but what is for fighting this Rebellion. Still, they will be glad to come back and live under the old flag. Last winter, after the Battle of Fredericksburg, the soldiers were most all discouraged, but they have great confidence in Gen Hooker. There is quite a number of Regiments that have served their time out & have gone home. A Regiment or two goes through here most every day. The third NY has gone home. The weather here is very warm & most of the time very pleasant but we have had a good deal of rain. The trees are leaved out & apple trees are in full blossom. We bought Col Tracy a sword, sash, spurs and shoulder straps that cost 208 dollars, & presented them to him. The company were marched up to the junction & were

The sword and scabbard, left, and detail of scabbard, right, presented to Captain Hyde. The engraving reads "Presented to Capt. R. H. S. Hyde Co. B, 109th Reg. N.Y.V. by his Comp'y. May 4/63." Collection of Michael Colella.

drawed up in line before his house. He was taken by surprise. It was quite affecting. He shed tears before he got through with his speech. The sword cost 150 dollars. It is most all silver with a little gold on the mountings. Our company paid for the whole of it. We also presented Captain Hyde with one that cost 62 dollars. I presume you will see an account of it in the Owego papers if you see them. I did not read McClellans trial. I presume he meant well enough but I think he was to slow. Hooker seems to be more of a fighting man. We are under Gen Heintzleman but I dont see any signs of our going to the front. You say they are going to have a canvas dance at Speedsville. I had not heard any thing about it. I dont hear from there very often now. A canvas dance is a dance they have under canvas out in the Park or any other good place such a canvas as they have to a barn. I think it must be lonesome with so many stars away as Hellen calls them especially with such stars as you & myself, but I think they will soon forget me. I presume if I should stay away a year or two longer they would forget that there ever was such a person as myself. I hope you will try & remember me if no one else. I will give you the praise of remembering me the best of any of my Speedsville friends so far. I hope you will continue for you may rest assured that I shall never, no never, forget you—not a day or hardly any hour has past but what you were in my thoughts. Our regiment were paid, four months pay, two weeks ago last Tuesday. Well my sheet is full & I must close.

With sincere regards for your future welfare, I remain your friend,

John
Address Washington, D.C.

Letter courtesy of the Berkshire Historian's Office.

Savage Switch. June 13th, /63

Dearest Friend;

I dont know as I ought to answer your letter so soon, but I guess I will be a good boy and may be next time you will answer sooner and besides all that, I must tell you about what a great battle we had last Thursday. We went up to the Junction as usual to drill on battallion, they having five companys stationed there. While the Lieut Col was drilling us about half a mile from the camp, orders came from the Col to bring the battalion down to camp immediately. When we were drawed up in line before him he spoke to us thus. "Soldiers of the 109th: the time for which you have so long looked for is about to come. The enemy has crossed the Potomac and are now advanceing on this railroad and

Bridge on Orange & Alexandria Railroad, Virginia. Library of Congress, Prints and Photographs.

we must prepare to meet them." He then dismissed us with orders to our Company to go back to Savage Switch and get everything ready for a fight. The Col had a telegraphic dispatch from Washington telling him to prepare for action. About one oclock a cannon was brought down here with grape and canister and stationed on the railroad near a very important bridge that we have guarded for the last six months. At two, the Colonel with four Companys came down with knapsacks all packed, ready for a march, fight or any thing else. One Company was sent out on picket and if they had come here they would have meet with a warm reception, but about three oclock a dispatch came saying that the Rebs had gone back across the river. So we were ordered back to camp again. So you see we had a great victory, if not a battle, because when they heard the 109th were ready for them, they skedaddled in a hurry! The Regt gave some of the heartys't cheers when they heard the Rebs were comeing you

Confederates crossing the Potomac. "It was believed that if General Lee were to cross the Potomac and enter Maryland thousands of young men would flock to his ranks; that Baltimore would welcome him with open arms; and that the possible result might be the capture of Washington, or a movement into Pennsylvania. ... The water was only knee-deep, and the soldiers swung their hats, cheered, and sung "Maryland! My Maryland!" Coffin, *Drum-Beat*, 298-9.

ever heard. The Lieut Col said "Boys lets have three cheers for the fight any way whether we have one or not." I tell you, we did not like it much because the Rebs did not come. We all asked for a fight. We wanted to show you folks up there that we are enough for the Rebs, if we are a band box Regt, as some of the folks up North call us. If we ever meet the enemy we will show you what the band box & pet Regt can do. The Rebels may recross the river again, but I dont believe they will dare to. The weather has been very dry here & is still. We have had no rain in a long time. Every thing is drying up. Captain Hyde has gone home for good. He tryed to get a trial to see if he could not get reinstated to his command again, but they would not grant him a trial, but he got his pay. He was dismissed for disloyalty, at least that was the charge, but I dont beleive he is disloyal. The charges were got up by some enemys of his. The boys felt pretty bad over it. They thought all the world of him. When we were called out and he talked to us there was not but a very few in the Company but what were crying. Lieut Wade is in command of the Company. I dont know wheather he will be Captain or not, but presume not. He is pretty good to the boys but he is not capable of the office. George Humphrey has got his discharge & gone home. The weather is warm and pleasant. We are not in cloth tents;

According to *The Owego Times*, as reprinted by the *Binghamton Daily Republican* of August 30, 1863, Captain Robert H. S. Hyde of the 109th assaulted an older man, W. S. Lincoln of Newark Valley. The incident took place at the Ahwaga House in Owego, New York. Hyde struck Lincoln several times and shouted "God d_m you, you black abolitionist, I'll kill you" and "Copperheads to the rescue," followed by "the vilest epithets his vocabulary could furnish." The newspaper continued, "Captain Hyde claims that he was dismissed from the service on certain charges preferred against him by

we are still in our barracks. What great stories has that soldier you spoke about been telling about what he has seen? Some of them tells a good many things. You need not send your letter in the care of any one. It will not come any safer.

Frank Bush wrote to me and told me to tell you to write to her. She says she has not had a letter from you in a long time but be sure and answer this first. I am very sorry for Del Jenks but it was good enough for him or any one else that wants to marry for money and nothing else. If they cannot really love a person they never ought to get married. This marring for money is not what it is cracked up to be. I think you done well to go to one meeting, about as well as myself since I have been down here. I went to a meeting last Sunday about three miles from here and guess I will go tomorrow. I went to a Negro meeting, to the first I ever attended, and of all the noises I ever heard, that beat them all! You would laugh to hear them. At the white meetings they all knew when the preacher prays. I would like to be at Speedsville the Forth first rate but I am to full of business. I hope you can read this, but I am afraid you cant. Write sooner than before.

John

Mr. Lincoln." The same newspaper, on September 2, reported that the charge against Hyde was that he used "disloyal and treasonable language." It claimed Hyde's lawyer tried to get the War Department to revoke his dismissal, but settled for Hyde's being allowed to resign, effective May 7, the date of his dismissal, in order to receive his back pay. The "Copperheads," or "Peace Democrats" as they called themselves, were antiwar. In this context, however, Hyde probably was referring to their stand against the President's Emancipation Proclamation as "wicked, inhuman, and unholy." James McPherson, "Introduction," in Paul Mathless and Henry Woodhead, editors. *1863: Turning Point of the Civil War.* (Alexandria, Virginia: Time-Life Books, 1998) 5. Newspaper excerpt, above, transcribed by John T. Goodnough from microfilm at the Broome County Public Library, Binghamton, New York, 2004, 2006.

A black revival meeting. *Frank Leslie's Illustrated Newspaper*, 1873. Courtesy of printsoldandrare.com.

Annapolis Junction. Sept. 27th, 1863

Friend Amelia,

I am going to direct this note to Speedsville. I think you
must be there by this time. If I remember right, you were
going to go home shortly after the sixteenth. I suppose you
are having a pleasant time there visiting your old friends.
I wish I was there. Dont you think Helen would forgive
me if I should come home and see her? I do. I dont think I
have done any thing very offensive. I have wrote to her and
explained the likeness affair to her satisfaction I hope. I dont
know but what I will have the pleasure of visiting Speedsville
while you are at home. They are now giveing furloughs again.
I have not applied for one yet but I am going to do so soon.
One has got a furlough filled out and two have gone home
with two of our boys that died last week. Henry Johnson died
Sunday, went home Monday. Theidore Dykeman, one that
married Alford Ford's daughter, died Wednesday & was sent
home Thursday. They both died with the typhoid fever. That
makes four that have died in this Co. since we came here. It
is quite sickly at presant. About 20 in the company are sick.
Mat Parker is sick in the hospital, but not dangerous. I will
try and get home about the middle of October. I dont expect
Lieut Wade will give me one. I shall go to the Col for it. The
weather is splendid but cold for this country. It is a good deal
colder than it was last year at this time. We have fixed up here
for the winter and will without doubt stay till spring.

I have attended the Temperance Lodge to Savage every
night but one since I joined. A great many have joined it
since I have. We elected officers last evening & I had the
honor of being elected Worthy Associate, the Secont office in
the lodge and run againset a citizen at that. There are a good
many good union folks in Savage, but I must say, they must
be pretty short of timber to put me in such an office as that,
dont you think so? I dont know what to think about Capt.

Hyde. I dont like his affair with Lincoln in Owego at all. He done wrong in strikeing Lincoln & I think lost a good many friends by it. You can say what you are a mind to about Capt now for what I care; he is not our Capt now nor never will be again. I wish I could say so by Wade. I suppose you would like to make folks beleive that I used to be pretty lazy, especily about getting up to breakfast. Now, I cannot hardly think you mean what you say for every one knows I am around at meal time if no other. If I remember right, a lady about your size used to get up rather late now and then. I hope though, you will not take any offence at what I say. I have got to be a very early riser. So much so, that I very often get up two or three times during the night to see if it is not most time for breakfast to be ready. I never miss breakfast here as I used to, as you say.

If I come home I guess I will have to get you to intercede with Helen for me, that is if I cannott make it all right, you would make a famous hand at that business. I liked to have forgot to tell you that the 11th and 12th Corps is passing through here on their way to Georgia to reinforce Gen Rosecrans at Chattanooga. They have ben going past here for the last two days. We expect the 137th along every hour. They will have a nice old ride before they get there. Excuse poor writing and also this short letter. From,

John

Robert Hyde returned home in May. On December 4, 1863, he was again sworn into the service, this time as Major of the 15th New York Cavalry.

"I very often get up two or three times during the night to see if it is not most time for breakfast to be ready." John. The next meal was frequently on soldiers' minds. Left and below, eating and drinking utensils. Collection of Michael Colella.

Headquarters, 109th NYSV

Falls Church, V.A.

October 21st, /63

Dear Friend,

I presume you will be surprised to see the heading of this letter for I had no idea my self of being here this evening. But it seems that I am not at Falls Church exacly but on the London and Hampshire Railroad, seven miles from Washington & seven from Alexandria. I left my sisters Wednesday night & reached Washington Thursday night at eleven oclock [returning from his furlough]. I took the street carr to Georgetown. Staid there till morning then crossed over on Masons Island & a Co of our Regt were there. The other two were left to guard the road at Laurel & Bladensburg. We were under marching orders again on Friday but did not leave till three oclock Sunday afternoon. We took three days rations, 40 rounds of cartridges & knapsacks full. We marched to Falls Church, a distance of seven miles. We got there at about eight oclock. Two companys were stationed at

Soldiers' Rest, Alexandria, Virginia, with boxcars in foreground. 1865. Library of Congress, Prints and Photographs. In October 1863 the regiment was ordered to Mason's Island, near Aqueduct Bridge over the Potomac River. A portion of the regiment, under the command of Lieutenant Colonel Isaac Swartwood Catlin of Owego, New York, was sent to Falls Church, Virginia, for duty. There, they guarded the Alexandria, Loudoun and Hampshire Railroad (south of Washington), which was not as strategically located as the Baltimore and Ohio). Taken from the Confederates in May 1861, the AL&H line helped to

a depot just beyond Falls Church, Col Tracy's Head Quarters. Two more were left two miles this side on the railroad. The other four companys marched Monday to where we are now, seven miles, I stood the march first rate. I like such soldiering better than laying still all the time. We did not have any thing to eat but hardtack & coffee excepting a very little raw pork. All we have now is bread and coffee but I think it is much better than what you gave me to eat when I came to see you. Dont you think so? Now, I am not runing down your baking at all but you know we are in the habit of having mule beef & all other good fixins down here. You must excuse me for to night, I must go to sleep. They expect the Rebels here to night. A dispatch came tonight to be ready for Mosby's Cavalry. He is expected to make a raid here to night. Good night and pleasant dreams.

John

supply garrisons defending the capital. It extended 30 miles to Leesburg, but its service was erratic. Confederate Colonel John S. Mosby and his 43rd Virginia Cavalry were guerrilla partisans operating behind Union lines beginning January 1863. "Mosby's Raiders" harassed and skirmished with Union soldiers and the AL&H Railroad, as well as other outposts, wagon trains, sentries and pickets until the end of the war.

October 22, 1863

I will now try and finnish this letter. We were called up at ten & taken to a fort about two miles from here. Four companys of us lay in ambush just outside of the fort near the road where the rebel guerrillas, to the number of one hundred, were expected to come. We lay there till daylight, then went home or to camp & never saw a Reb. We all liked to froze to death. The fort is not occupied but is a very strong position. One thousand men would stand a pretty heavy force. It seems that Mosebys men got inside of our lines and there was'nt but three or four different roads for them to get out of and they were all strongly guarded. Three of them were guarded by our own Regt. I have not heard wheather they had a brush with them or not. We are encamped within a mile of Nepton Hill. I presume you have heard of the place before. It is merely a fort on a hill. McCllens Army encamped all over the hills, before he went to Richmond or near there.

We have got a new captain, Edward Evans, the one I heard

John S. Mosby (center, white pants) and men. *The Photographic History of The Civil War in Ten Volumes: Volume Four, The Cavalry* (New York: The Review of Reviews Co., 1911) 171.

had got a commission when I was to home. He makes a good one so far. The boys like him first rate, a good deal better then Lieut Wade. I dont know how long we will stay on this road. I think we will stay till all the wood's carried through. They have got a lot of wood to run through. They have not run on this railroad before since last spring. They commenced running Monday morning.

I have not got your letter you wrote me yet. I guess it has miscarried, but if it has it is the first one. I never have lost a letter before as I know of. I guess you will have to write me annother one now to make up for that. Write and tell me what a time you had to your party, who were there and all about it. I would have liked to have ben there very much. I think, however, it was excusable under the circumstances. I should certainly have staid if it had not ben for seeing my sister. I guess I have wrote enough, such as it is. I dont know as you can read it. Write soon, give my respect to all.

With sincere regards to your welfare, I remain your truest friend.

John

Upton Hill. November 20th, 1863

Dear Friend,

It was with the greatest pleasure that I perused your letter of the fifteenth for I had almost come to the painful conclusion that you had entirely forsaken me. Almost six weeks without one word! Only think of what suspense I must have ben in, in a land full of rebels and guerrillas, expecting every minute to be my [last]. Now Amelia, dont you think you ought to ask my forgiveness and be a real good girl, as you are & write often? When you go to war I will write every day. I am not making great promises, I guess not more than I can fulfill, although I believe you once agreed to go if I would. But, never mind. I will forgive all past offenses if you will only be true to promises in the future. Two companies have moved back on the island. The roads are in good order for the army to move. I dont suppose we will ever go in front, at least not as long as there is a railroad to guard. I enjoy soldiering here very well. I cannot say I like it anywhere, nor did not expect to when I enlisted. I think I would enjoy marching the best, if I could stand it. No doubt but what you would like to have me live on hardtack all the time, but Uncle Abraham looks out for his boys. We now have the best kind of bread and applesauce besides. Aint he generous? I did not think you were so cruel as to want a soldier to live on hardtack. About 500 of our Regt have ben home to vote. I should have went home if I had not just ben home. I might have went if I had of known how things were working. All those that went to the colonel went home. I suppose

Letter courtesy of Marian Gallagher, Maine, New York.

Hardtack was a staple of the Union Army soldier's diet. The biscuits were so hard when issued they had to be soaked to a mush before they could be eaten. After being carried in the field for awhile, however, they became moldy and infested with insect larvae. The soldiers called them "worm castles." George Worthington Adams. *Doctors in Blue: The Medical History of the Union Army in the Civil War* (Baton Rouge: Louisiana State University Press, 1996) 208. Below, vintage hardtack. Collection of Michael Colella.

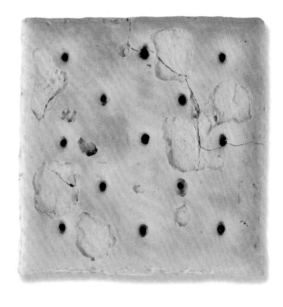

they had a gay old time. They took an extra train. They got to Owego on Sunday, marched through the streets to the Awaga House where they had a good dinner prepared for them. They came pretty near destroying Bebees Printing Office & probably would have ben if it had not ben for Hatfield, Gruman & some others. They urged them not to do it. He came out with an article abusing the soldiers, charging they were pledged to vote for the Republicans ticket. There was'nt a man there that pledged himself to vote for any ticket. There

Soldiers of the 109th New York Volunteers, left to right, pages 90-91: Gus Chittenden, Company D; Royal Rosbrooks, Company A; Martin Gissnan, Company C; Abram Van Gorder, Company D; Leroy Chittenden, Company D; Lucion Crandell, Company D.

wasn't a word said about voting either way. They took almost every vote in this Company & lots of Democrats voted the union ticket. I presume there was not more than twenty-five out of five-hundred that voted the Democratic ticket. I hope they will remember us soldiers on Thanksgiving, but I presume they will not. Some of them dont like our style. There is no Regiment guarding the Washington & Baltimore but two companies of our Regt. Companies G and K are there yet. I cannot hardly stand it not having any lodge to attend or pretty girls to see, but I guess I will live through it.

John suggests that men like these from his regiment went back to New York State to vote and that they likely were nearly unanimous in supporting President Lincoln's candidacy. Photographs, collection of Michael Colella.

Lieut Rightmire has resigned and gone home. When I got back here, it was reported that I had got married when I was home. Someone wrote to one of the boys, Joel Allen, to that effect. I guess it was his wife that wrote it and who do you suppose it was to? Cant you guess? It seems they know more about it than I do. What do you think about it?

I dont know as you can read this so I will close.

John Tidd

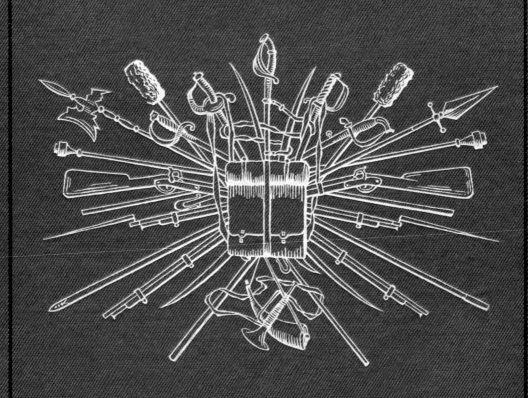

The Furnace Roar of the Battle

There was an ominous, clanging overture to the charge when the shafts of the bayonets rattled upon the rifle barrels. At the yelled words of command the soldiers sprang forward in eager leaps. There was new and unexpected force in the movement of the regiment. … The men scampered in an insane fever of haste, racing as if to achieve a sudden success before an exhilarating fluid should leave them. It was a blind and despairing rush by the collection of men in dusty and tattered blue, over a green sward and under a sapphire sky, toward a fence, dimly outlined in smoke, from behind which sputtered the fierce rifles of enemies.

—Stephen Crane, *The Red Badge of Courage*, 1895

With the exception of two occasions—first, a June 13, 1863, order to stop Confederates who reportedly were poised to threaten the Baltimore & Ohio Railroad and to cut the telegraph lines between Baltimore and Washington, and second, an order to lie in wait to ambush Mosby's Cavalry, reportedly on a raid near Falls Church, Virginia, during the night of October 21 and 22, 1863 (neither anticipated skirmish came to pass)—the men of Company B and the 109th had idled more than 15 months as "the band box railroad regiment," spending dreary, boring hours on uneventful guard duty.

In mid-January 1864, the company was sent to the Soldier's Rest in Alexandria, Virginia. New responsibilities had the company guarding conscripts and volunteers and providing escort duty to the soldiers' regiments.

All that was about to change. John's letter to Amelia dated April 2, 1864, reported routine guard duty, but hinted that rumors were swirling regarding Company B's imminent departure for the front. Early in March, President Lincoln promoted

Illustration created from the cover of Charles Carleton Coffin, *Freedom Triumphant* (New York: Harper & Brothers, 1891).

Major General U. S. Grant to lieutenant general (a rank previously held only by George Washington), with the approval of Congress. Grant became the General in Chief of all Federal Armies. One of his first acts was to reorganize the Army of the Potomac into three infantry corps: the 2nd, 5th, and 6th, plus one cavalry troop under Major General Philip H. Sheridan. The 1st and the 3rd Corps were eliminated and their soldiers transferred to other corps. The 9th, to which John and his comrades were assigned, was under the separate command of General Ambrose Burnside.

Until then, the Union Armies had fought without close coordination. They usually were slow to engage in battle and reluctant to keep fighting once a battle had been fought. This permitted the Confederates to rest, restock arms and supplies, replenish manpower losses, train new soldiers, and move freely from place to place. Lt. General Grant had a reputation for winning battles. He also had a different philosophy concerning how the war could be won: "From an early period in the rebellion I had been impressed with the idea that active and continuous operations of all the troops that could be brought into the field, regardless of season and weather, were necessary to a speedy termination of the war. The resources of the enemy and his numerical strength were far inferior to ours; but as an offset to this, we had a vast territory, with a population hostile to the Government, to garrison, and long lines of river and railroad communications to protect, to enable us to supply the operating armies."

Lt. General U. S. Grant. William Swinton, *Campaigns of the Army of the Potomac* (New York: Charles B. Richardson, 1866) frontispiece.

U. S. Grant, *O.R.* 36(2) 3.

Lee's forces were south of the Rapidan River in Virginia, defending Richmond. General Joseph E. Johnson's troops were guarding Atlanta, a very important Rebel rail and supply center. Grant's objectives were to capture and subdue both armies and the cities they defended. William T. Sherman, Grant's commander of the Union Army in the west, led 100,000 men toward Atlanta in early May.

After three-and-a-half months of guarding and escorting new soldiers, Company B of the 109th moved to Annapolis, Maryland, where they joined other companies. On April 26, the men were ready for whatever lay ahead. By May 1, they were truly on the march, now identified as part of the 1st Brigade, 3rd Division, 9th Corps under General Burnside, who, as did everyone in the Union Army, now answered to Grant. The ordinary men cared little for organization and reorganization. The important thing was that 19 months of guard duty were behind them. They were heading into confrontations with the Rebs at last!

John's 1864 diary survived and was found in a Berkshire, New York, home—not far from Speedsville. This chapter will supplement his letters with diary entries, used by permission of the Berkshire Historian's Office, along with selected excerpts from the writing of others.

Lt. General U. S. Grant immediately assumed direction of the campaign in Virginia and established his headquarters with the Army of the Potomac, commanded by General Meade. Grant accompanied this army and directed its maneuvers. Because of bad weather and poor road conditions, operations had been delayed until May 1. James Williams of the 109th, in a May 15 letter home from a camp two miles from Fredericksburg, wrote: "You have probably seen an account of some of the fighting of the 109th here. We have been the despised regiment on account of being so long on the Baltimore and Ohio Railroad. Those days are past and we are now serving our country in a different and more dangerous way. We have already seen a short battle of 10 days and the hardest battle that ever was fought. … Our army thus far has met with great success. We have not as yet met with a single defeat. … I believe the days are beginning to dawn when the rebellion shall be forgotten."

not care for either of them after I receive
your answer to this I am sure I shall
not if you written me. Orderly Sergeant
Nelson has been appointed Second Lieut
of our Company in place of Lieut Righ=
mire.   We had an Oyster dinner for
our Christmas we took the Company funds
& bought enough for the whole Company, it
cost for all, Oysters, Butter. Crackers & Cigars
31 dollars. we have over 100 dollars Company
funds.   Mosebys Guerrillas haven't troubled
us much yet. & don't beleive he will, some
of C. A. boys fired three guns at a
man the other night that they supposed
was one of Mosebys Guerrillas they never
hit him however, he took to his heels
About 800. of Stuarts Cavalry came to
Fairfax Station about 12 miles from
here a Short time ago, but they were dri=
=en off. I hear that they will not muster
Captain Hyde into the service again
I should not be surprised if they did not.

[Around New Years 1864]

...not care for eather of them after I received your answer to this. I am sure I shall not if you written me. Orderly Sergeant Nelson has been appointed Secont Lieut of our Company in place of Leient Rightmire. We had an Oyster dinner for our Christmas. We took the Company funds & bought enough for the whole company. It cost for all, Oysters, Butter, Crackers & Segars, 31 dollars. We have over 100 dollars Company funds. Mosebys Guerrillas have'nt troubled us much yet. I dont beleive he will. Some of Co. A. boys fired three guns at a man the other night that they supposed was one of Mosebys Guerrillas—they never hit him however, he took to his heels. About 800 of Stuarts Cavelry came to Fairfax Station about 12 miles from here a short time ago, but they were driven off. I hear that they will not muster Captain Hyde into the service again. I should not be surprised if they did not. I guess they will have to draft. I dont beleive they can get vollenteers enough. It seems hard to take men when they dont want to go, but it is no worse for them than me or any one else. They have got the Small Pox on the Island & they are afraid it will get into the Regt generaly. It started from a conscript that we were guarding. The Doctors are vacainating the whole Regt. Our Company were vaccineated yesterday. I am doing guard duty for my happy New Year. I am on the Railroad two miles from camp & close by a Contraband Camp of Negroes. All the Negroes that escape from slavery find a home there; they work a large farm that the Government confiscated. I had a letter from George Witmore night before last. He says Tom Olney turned Albion Watkins out of school, because he would not read a composition. Tom told him to read it—he said he wouldn't do it, Tom then told him to take his books and leave, & he done so.

The roads are all mud—it has been quite rainy for the

Sarah Palmer ("Aunt Becky") was stationed near Washington during this epidemic. She wrote, "We had small-pox in our hospital at Mason's Island, and the pest-house to which they were taken proved in almost every instance the dead-house also." S. A. Palmer, *Aunt Becky's Army-Life*, 42.

Bridge over the Potomac. Johnson, Ridpath, and others, *Campfire and Battlefield*, 22.

past few days. Our Armys will not be able to move again this winter; in fact, there dont seem to be any fighting any where at presant. There is'nt but a few but what thinks this war, will end before next June. I dont beleive it will close quite as soon as that, but the Rebellion is fast caving in, the sooner the war ends the better it will sute me. Excuse mistakes & poor writing for my pen is poor. Hoping to hear from you soon.

I remain your dearest friend,

John. Tidd
Co. B. 109th Regt. N.Y.V.
Washington, D.C.

Soldier's Rest, Alexandria V.A.
January 18th 1864

Dear Friend Amelia,

I perused your letter invain for the answer to my question which I think you ought to answer one way or the other; however, I think you like me a little, just a very little, perhaps enough to think of me when you get homesick & have nothing else to think of. You probably know what you have written to me as well as my-self, you have'nt written anything very criminal—but you were quite provoking sometimes. I suppose I shall have to forgive you if you will promise to do better in future. I did not injoy myself very well New Years as you thought. I was on guard, and it was a dreadful cold day, as cold as we have in New York. I wished a good many times I were in Speedsville; if you could have been there I would have enjoyed it very much. If you will get an Ambrotype taken on tin & send to me; I will send this back & thank you ever so much; you can sent it in a letter. I like them the best, they always look more like the original. How can you say, "if I care for it," you know I do. I have headed this letter, Soldier's Rest, but I am not there to day.

I am in camp, about one mile & ahalf from the City of Alexandrea, Virginia. I have been on duty at the Soldiers Rest in the City for the past two days guarding Conscripts and Vollenteers. You may be surprised to hear of our being here after going into winter quarters. We had marching orders for five Companys of our Regt. on the 8th but did not leave till the 12th, last Tuesday; we packed all of our things up & took them to the Railroad in the morning & waited there till 4 oclock before the cars came. We got to Alexandria or to our camp about sundown; unloaded our bagage & got on the train & rode back to the City, to the Soldier's Rest & staid till Friday afternoon. We releived the 4th Delawere Regiment which has gone to Fairfax Court House & had to wait for

In early 1864 John wrote that the Rebellion was "fast caving," unaware that some of the most fierce chapters were about to be written. J. T. Headley. *The Great Rebellion; A History of Civil War in the United States* (Connecticut: American Publishing Co., 1866).

them to go away so we could encamp on their ground. We are tented on the ground, which is just as muddy as it can be. We have a few boards to sleep on that we brought along—if had not of brought any with us we would have had to sleep in the mud. Our business is to guard Conscripts & Vollenteers to their

Camped within "80 rods" of the Potomac, John saw vessels of all types "constantly running up & down the River." A rod is 5.5 linear yards. Photograph by Mathew Brady. Collection of Tioga County Historical Society.

Regiments wherever they enlist for & guard them while they are here. About 1,900 are here already & more comeing every day. Eight men from each Company started for the front with a lot of men yesterday morning. Annother lot of men are detailed to start to night with some more. We may have to take some to Tennessee; all of the New York boys will come here, then I may have the chance of guarding them. They are not allowed to leave the room without a guard, Vollenteers or Conscripts. Some of them stay here two or three weeks.

Three Companys of our Regt. are on Masons Island, guarding Conscripts & two are on the Washington & Baltimore Branch Railroad. Col. Catlin is in command of us & he is under Gen. Brigs. We eat at the Soldiers Relief while we are on guard. A thousand men can sit down at once. Our Camp is within 80 rods of the Potomac & 20 of the Railroad. I should have written before this time but I have had no time; I have been buisy all the time till to day & I have no more time now. Excuse the writing for my pen & ink are miserble. Write soon.

A conscript was one taken by lot from the conscription list and compelled to serve as a soldier or sailor—a person who had been drafted and did not pay $300 to be excused or who did not provide a substitute.

John
Address as before

:, .   Camp Briggs, Alexandria, VA
February 6th 1864

Friend Amelia,

Your ever welcome letter came to hand on Wednesday Eve
& where do you suppose your humble servent was about that
time—I presume you could not guess. I was to the Theatre
in Alexandria. It was an Indian peice that they acted—it was
splendid too. It is the first I ever attended. The weather is
warm and pleasant without any snow; it has been as warm as
summer. We are encamped within 80 rods of the Potomac.
It will be quite pleasant in the summer. Vessels of all sizes are
constantly runing up & down the River.

The Capitol & Washington are in full view of our camp,
it is only seven miles off. Alexandria is about as large as
Binghamton. Washington is as large as three of it. I have
been down in front as far as Warrenton Village once &
twice at Warrenton Junction within 15 miles of Gen Meads
headquarters & 8 of the Rappahannock. It is about 50
miles from Alexandria & 70 to Culpepper Court House.
Some of our boys have been to the Rapidan so they could
see the Rebel camps. I am in hopes I shall get a chance to
go to Culpepper next time I go off for I want to go and see
the 76th Regt. They are stationed about a mile from there;
two or three of our boys have been there. Some of our boys
have been to Tennessee with some and to Fortress Monroe
& the Companys on Mason Island took 27 of the Maryland
Conscripts to Wisconsin to join Gen Pope to fight the
Indians. The Volenteers are comeing in every day & are sent
to their Regiments as fast as they come. We receive them at
the Warfs, take them to the Soldiers Rest—there are two of
them. There we guard them till they are armed, which we do;
then we guard them to their Regiments. We have charge of
all the Volenteers & Conscripts from N.Y, Penn, N.J., MD,
De, & all of the New England States. The three Companys

Warrenton was the center
of operations north of the
Rappahannock.

on Masons Island guard the Conscripts from Maryland.
We have more duty to do than any other Regiment in the
field & as responsible duty as there is & are in full as much
danger as those in front at the presant time. We very often
have to walk eight or ten miles through places where there
are plenty of Guerrillas and the cars are not very safe to ride
on by any means. They run off the track and run into one
other & smash things up most beautifuly and once awhile a
train is fired into by Guerrillas. A train was fired into by ten
Guerrillas only about a mile from Alexandria but no one was
hurt; that was done last Sunday night. Our boys were not on
the train. The 83rd Penn guard the forage trains. Deserters

One advantage the North
had over the South was a
much larger population,
and the ability to continue
to enlist fresh recruits. The
109th guarded the new
recruits until they were
outfitted and transported to
their regiments. Illustration
of Union and Confederate
Army uniforms. Calvin D.
Cowles, George B. Davis,
Joseph W. Kirkley, Leslie
J. Perry. *War Department
Atlas to accompany the of-*

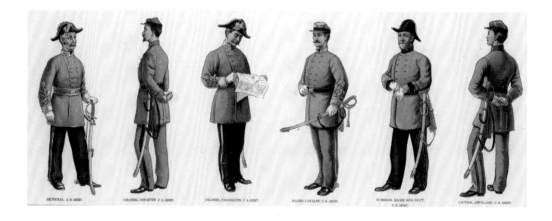

come into our lines at the rate of ten or twelve a day. Six Rebel Cavalry came into our lines at the first station from here the other day with horses & every thing & delivered themselves up; they came here, took the oaths & were set at liberty—they were real smart looking fellows. One man came here last Friday—he came from Alabama; he was Conscripted & taken to Richmond, staid with the Regt 13 days & run away. He said he walked four days barefooted—he was when he came into camp at least. The boys gave him a pair of shoes, hat and pants. He kept away from them for two months by laying in the mountains till it got so cold he could stand it no longer. Then he went home and was taken. I think there will

ficial records of the Union and Confederate armies (Washington: Government Printing Office, 1895) pl. CLXXII. David Rumsey Map Collection, www.davidrumsey.com.

be a grand time among the Rebs when their three year troops time are out which will be in the spring. The Rebel Congress have passed a bill keeping the troops in the field and not to discharge them when their time is out. They say they will [not] fight but what will go home & desert to our lines in a body. They have already disbanded two Regiments because they would not obey orders. In a South Carolina Regt they undertook to desert in a body, the whole Regt, but got wind off it & shot 20 of the leaders & distributed the rest among other Regiments.

I think they will see all they want too of the Yankees before next fall & be glad to return to the arms of Uncle Abraham. It is the prevailing opinion among every one that the war will not last longer than this next summer. I guess Honest Old Abe will have to serve annother four years in the Presidents

Deserters entering the Union lines. "… thousands in the Confederate ranks were beginning to see that theirs was a hopeless cause, and were asking themselves why such a sacrifice of life, for what were they fighting? … Every day there were desertions from the Confederate ranks,

Hall Chair. He will receive my vote at least & two thirds of the Army. There is a good many Grant men, but they think he will do better where he is. They are now drawing lumber for Barracks for these five companys. They are going to build them large enough to hold a whole company of 150 men; they are building the same on Masons Island. I presume we will stay here all next summer. Col. Tracy has got an order from the War department to fill the 109th Regt up to 1500 men & Quartermaster Hopkins is now at Elmira for the

those on picket throwing down their guns and entering the Union lines." Charles Carleton Coffin, *Redeeming the Republic* (New York: Harper & Brothers, 1890) 243, 249.

purpose of getting recruits. Now is the time to enlist in the best Regiment in service. No other Regt is allowed over 1,000 men. Some say we are going to be transfered into heavy artillery in the spring and go into forts around Washington & Baltimore. I should not wonder if it was so for 1500 are allowed in that branch of service. All of our sick men have gone to the Invalid Corps, Frank Taylor with the rest. Most all of our Regt have been sick with colds. I have got the worst one I have had since I have been a soldier but have been on duty all the time. An Orderly Sergeant just deserted from the Rebs. Says he saw more men killed for the number engaged the other day then in any battle since the war & all among themselves. Two Mississippi Regiments revolted & under took to desert to our lines when they ordered the artillery, infantry, & cavalry to fire into them, which they did & almost massacred them. I presume you read about our pickets hearing some very heavy fireing among the Rebs a few days ago. I have not heard from Hellen or Frank Bush in most of three months but it is not my fault. I wrote last & never write two letters without receiving any answer, unless I think it did not reach its destination. I heard of Willoughbys marriage through a letter from George Nixon & I think he has done much better then to have had the other one—you no who. And by the way, Nixon has got a little girl and A. Phillips a young soldier. All of the boys from NY will come here first before they go to their Regiments. I do like an ambrotype the best, so remember me. It is almost Valentine day. I wonder if I will get any. I will have to stop for my sheet is full. If you read this, you will do well. Take good care of yourself and [do] not work to hard.

　Your friend,

John Tidd

Model 1861 rifle, .58 caliber. Collection of Michael Colella.

Camp Briggs, Alexandria, V.A.
March 5th, 1864

Friend Amelia,

Well, here I am again; how do you do this rainy afternoon? But I forget that it dont always rain up there when it does here. It does rain here but it is quite warm, it will soon be warm weather again. We are still on the ground. Our barracks are not more than half done yet & will not be done before April. They are going to build a cook house large enough for the whole five companys to eat in. I should not be surprised if we staid here all next summer. We are fixing up as though we were going to stay here during the war. We have had plenty of business now days. I went of last Monday with recruits for the front—went to Brandy Station, from there went afoot through the mud & rain about five miles & back. Went to the headquarters of the 1st Div of the 3rd Army Corps & about the same distance to other parts of the Army from Brandy. I got back to camp on Thursday. Was'nt in camp two hours before I was detailed to take three men to Fort Baker, Washington. I took the boat—delivered the men, staid in the Washington Rest all night, took the boat the next morning,

Because the 109th was building barracks at Camp Briggs, John speculated that he would remain there through the summer. In fact, the 109th headed for the front in April. Photograph of men constructing barracks, from Johnson, Ridpath, and others, *Campfire and Battlefield*, 350.

came back yesterday & have been in camp since. I have been
right past Gen Meads tent—he lives in a common wall tent. I
did not have the honor of seeing him once. Gen. Briggs says
we are doing more duty, these five companys, than any other
whole Regiment. I know we are on duty most all the time. I
came pretty near going to Fort Monroe Thursday. I happened
to be up to Co. & so they took some one else in my place.
I presume we will be in this business all summer. I see they
have put off the draft till April. I should think they could
raise the men by that time. The Army has been moving some
lately. The 6th Corps & a part of the 3rd crossed the Rapidan
while Gen. Killpatrick made a dash on Richmond. He has
failed in the attempt to take it but he tore up about 40 miles
of Railroad, blowed up Bridges, Mills, & c &c. Frank Taylor
has got his discharge; is going home in a few days. A lot of
new recruits came in for this Regt but were most all sent
back to Masons Island to be examined over again. They dont
like their looks. I suppose they think up north that they
can put any kind of men into our Regt but they will find
themselves mistaken. I had a letter from Frank Bush. They
were all going to move to Candor. I dont see how Helen and

Tearing up the railroads.
Morton, *Sparks from the
Camp Fire*, 247.

Frank can stand it to live away from Speedsville. I know it from experience. I have'nt received any Valentines this year. In fact—I never got one in my life, on[ly] what I bought. I wonder who did send you that Valentine? It must have been sent by Uncle Abe. I dont see who it could have been if not him. Yes, I will certainly escort you & Franc to the theater if you will come & see me. I think the folks around there are mistaken for the heavy artillery is the best branch of service there is unless they like active service. There is not much danger in artillery, they are in forts mostly but I guess we will not be transferred into artillery this spring. I have no dought but what I would be used first rate if I could come out there the 11th & would give a good deal to come but you will have to excuse me this time.

No more at present,

Good bye / John Tidd

Soldier's Rest, Alexandria, V.A.
April 2nd, 1864

Dear Friend,

I received your ever welcome letter last Wednesday evening but had so much to do that I could not get time to answer till this evening. Therefore, I trust you will pardon me for not answering immediately. Was on duty Wednesday, Thursday and yesterday and last night so you can judge how much I feel like writing to night. I am off of duty to day & night. It commenced raining last night & has rained till now & it is still raining very hard. It snowed about half the day to day. I never saw such cold rainy weather this time of year in Speedsville. I rec'ed your letter; the one before this & would have answered right off but I knew you would receive my letter that I had written about three days before & so I did not write you. Our Company have been detached from the other four companys for the purpose of doing all the guard duty at the Soldiers Rest. We come on duty now every other day. When not on duty we stay in our tents outside of the fence that surrounds the Rest; but have to eat in the eating room of the Rest. The living is miserble. Salt fat pork boiled, not fit for a dog to eat, bread & a mixture of coffee about

Winter quarters, City Point, Virginia. c. 1861-1865. Library of Congress, Prints and Photographs.

like dishwater. We have the same every morning & night.
For dinner we have some kind of soup, but that is nothing
to what I expect we will have when we go to the front. It has
been rumored for three or four days past that we were going
to the front. Col Catlin says to day that we were surely going
away. He is going to send his wife home & the other mens
wifes that are here. I dont believe we will go, but still we may
for they are takeing most all the soldiers that have been laying
around Washington & putting Invalids in their places. Some
think we will leave within a week but do not be alarmed till
you know for certain that we have taken Richmond. We have
been staying here so long it seems almost impossible that we
will ever go. I did not laugh at you for being so anxious about
me for fear I was sick. I am sure I should feel full as anxious
about you if I should hear you were sick—and besides it
shows that there is one of Uncle Sams boys at least who has
made an impression on your heart. Oh! Amelia, shall we
ever be able to see Mrs. Reed & family again if they go West.
Speedsville is almost desolate & may be quite by the time this
cruel war is over.

The Veteran Reserve Corps (VRC), first known as the Invalid Corps, was established to guard supply depots, prison camps and other areas, freeing able-bodied men to go to the front.

I had quite an accident happen the other day or rather I
was along. I took charge of 25 recruits with four guards to go
to Vienna. We got on the cars, flat bottom ones. They started
to back up here. They got about two miles [and] the cars
struck a cow—throwed two cars off the track that was coverd
with Negroes. You ought to see them jump! Some went under
them & in all direcktions but no one was hurt much. The car
we were on was the only one that did'nt run off. So of course
we came back & coming back the engine killed annother cow.
I have'nt had any maple sugar or eggs this spring; excuse, I
had some eggs to an eating house—buckwheat cakes & other
fixins.

Write soon as convenient and I will remain your
affectionate friend.

John

Camp "Near" Alexandria, VA

April 27, 1864

Friend Amelia,

We are now on the tented field & encamped between 30,000 or 40,000 troops. Burnsides Corps one division has passed us already. Seven batterys of Artillery of six guns each, in all forty-two pieces & one Regiment of Cavalry have passed & lay waiting, expect for transportation to Fortress Monroe. There is two or three more divisions between here & Washington. Where we are camped there is about four thousand men with our Regt. We are to be formed into a brigade and join Gen Burnside. They say we are going into the 3rd Division, dont know yet what brigade. There is ten thousand Negro troops in the Corps. Our Regiment are all here & about one mile from Alexandria. I dont know where we are going but presume we will go to Fortress Monroe & from there to Richmond with Gen Butlers forces. We will have an Army of about seventy five thousand men. If Gen Grant holds Gen Lee in front, I think we will be in Richmond by the middle of May. The 109th are at last going into active service. I think Col. Tracy will be Brigadier General before long if he lives. Some day he is going to be acting Brigadier General. What will they think of Col. Tracys going in the field now? The folks up North said he would resign if he has to go to [the] front. Excuse all mistakes and poor writing for we are in shelter tents and it is a poor place to write. If you should not hear from me again in two months, you need not be alarmed for all mails are stoped below Alexandria for two months. I cannot write any more, So good by. From your loving friend,   John Tidd

Continued—Three days rations are in our Haversacks & an extra pair of shoes. We have to take 140 rounds of cartridges; 40 in our cartridge boxes and the rest in wagons and twenty days rations; five with us, the rest are carried. I am going to throw my overcoat away when we go on a march. J.T.

The U.S. Army Heritage and Education Center, Carlisle, Pennsylvania, part of the Winey Collection.

"Locked in Fearful Strife."
Morton, *Sparks from the
Camp Fire*, 95.

[Authors' note: Between John's letter of April 27, 1864, and his next letter of June 20, 1864, almost two months passed without communication between John and Amelia. During this time the 109th moved to the front and engaged in many battles. The following pages present John's diary entries from these months.]

April 27—Marched about a mile and encamped with three other Regiments who we are going to brigade with. A whole division of Burnsides Corps were kepted here for transportation to Fort Monroe & baterys of 6 guns each. We took three days rations. It is a hot day. We have shelter tents.

April 28—Started at 11 oclock, marched to Fairfax Court House. Reached there at seven oclock. It was a dusty hot day. Marched 15 miles.

April 28—The 109th was ordered to join the 9th Army

After guarding railroads around Washington and conducting new volunteers and conscripts to their regiments at the front, the 109th was ordered to join the 9th Corps, assembling at Annapolis, Maryland. On April 26, 1864, the 109th left Annapolis for the front.

Crops, under Burnside, which was to form a portion of General Grant's Army.

April 29—Marched to Mannas Junction 16 miles. It is hot & dusty. Three of our company were left at Fairfax Court House this morning. They gave out. Col Tracy is with us.

April 30—Started at seven, reached Warrenton Junction at half past four, distance 10 miles. It is hot & dusty. It rained a little just at night. I stood the march first rate. A very few fell out on the march to day.

May 1—Marched one half mile beyoynd Warrenton Junction and camped near the division headquarters. I joined our Brigade 1 1/2 miles which is 1st Brigade, 3rd Division, 9th Corps. It is warm & pleasant.

May 2—It is cloudy and cool. Staid in camp all day. The men not able to carry knapsacks turned in their guns. Battalion drill to day.

May 3—It is pleasant but cool. Had Brigade inspection. Orders were read on dress parade that our division would resume its march at 7 oclock. Took 6 days rations.

May 4—Marched to Rappahannock, crossed the river & camped about an hour then were ordered to strike tents and march one mile & formed in line of battle. Staid a while then retreated back to our old camp. Read four letters. It is hot & dusty. Our brigade took the lead of the division. Marched 14 miles.

May 5—Marched at 5 oclock, crossed the Rappedan at 12 p.m. We got to the Rebel picket lines at one p.m. 21 miles. Laid in line till 7, than went on picket within sight of their lines. General Grant's pickets are skirmishing; can hear them plainly. A great many fell and then fell dead in our Brigade. Hot and dusty.

May 6—Marched four miles & laid in a peice of woods. They shelled the woods & wounded five of our men. Went two miles further & formed in line of battle and commenced fireing on the Rebs. Made three charges. Our men killed two

On May 4, Union forces crossed the Rappahannock River and entered "the Wilderness," a densely thicketed, thorny area in central Virginia. Grant planned a quick forced march through that scrubland in order to place his army between Lee's Confederates and Richmond. Lee divined Grant's strategy and determined to stop the Army of the Potomac in the Wilderness. The battle commenced May 5.

On May 6, John's Company B and the 109th began a line of march into the Wilderness and came under fire near Wilderness Tavern. Captain Edwin Evans wrote that his men returned fire "vigorously and with considerable effect. After receiving the enemy's fire for a few moments, we were ordered to a charge, and moved at a double-quick upon the enemy, driving him from a line of works, taking some, killing and wounding quite a number of the enemy, and sustaining a loss in killed and wounded of not far from 60 men." Company B was relieved at 3:30 p. m., its ammunition spent. E. Evans, *O.R.*, S1, V36(1), 961.

"The woods are thick with killed and wounded. … The last year's leaves are like tinder. They take fire, and the flames sweep over the ground between the lines. The wounded cry for help. Some are snatched from the flames, but for others there is no relief." Coffin, *Redeeming the Republic*, 88-89.

In the Battle of the Wilderness fires raged, started by small arms fire and artillery. Wounded men unable to move and beyond assistance were burned to death. Many wounded who did not die in the Wilderness fire were doomed anyway. Only those able to stand a long jolting journey in 813 wagons and ambulances were loaded on May 7. They moved with the army during the night toward Spotsylvania, a dozen miles away. Some 960 other wounded were left behind. Most died from their wounds and lack of food and supplies. Lee was waiting for Grant's army behind strong entrenchments in Spotsylvania. John's unit was rear guard during the May 8 and 9 battle. By May 10, Company B advanced. Captain Edwin Evans related: "Sixty men were detailed

Rebs to our one and took prisoners. We lost in killed and wounded about 75 men. Had nothing to eat for two days but hardtack. Hot and dry.

May 7—Built breast works of trees & lay in wait for the rebs to advance on us. Is hot but pleasant. Lay there till one at night then we advanced toward Fredericksburg. We did not sleep any tonight.

May 8—Laurel Hill/Po River. Marched 9 miles, two beyond Chancellorsville & encamped for the night. Had five more days rations dealt out to us. It is very hot & dusty. I gave out and fell to the rear. Didnt sleep much.

May 9—Marched five miles & had to stop & fight the rebels. Hot and dusty.

May 10—Built breastworks and lay still all day. Twards night the shells flew all around & we lay flat on our bellies, then went into the woods. Got tangled all up, finally got straightaned all right. Jerome Rodney was wounded today.

May 11— Marched up in line of battle into an open field & lay in the rain & mud exposed to the shells & bullets all day. At four oclock we charged on the Rebel works. The shells

& grape shot flew a perfect hurricane!

May 12—We had to break & run. Out of six companys we lost about one hundred twenty five killed, wounded and prisoners. It was awful to behold! The greatist slaughter of the war! Nothing to eat all day.

May 13—Dug intrenchments & lay in the mud & rain exposed to the Rebel sharp shooters. I laid all night in the mud and rain with nothing under or over me. Mustered 21 men today.

May 14—Lay exposed to Rebel sharp shooters all day. Two of our boys wounded. Considerable rain. It rained some to night. I lay in the mud and rain without any thing under or over me. Two of our Regt were wounded, one in Company K & H.

as skirmishers, and thrown forward at a double-quick under a heavy shell fire, followed by the battalion. Skirmish line captured a light line of works of recent construction where the battalion spent the night." He continued, "Broke camp at an early hour, again crossed the Ny River, formed in line of battle, and maneuvered until near 10 a.m., when we were assigned to support a battery for an hour. We moved across fields, formed in line of battle and lay under shell fire until 1 p.m., when we were ordered to make a steady advance upon the enemy and find him. By misunderstanding of orders, our regiment charged upon his works. We sustained a heavy loss in killed, wounded, and prisoners. We could not take his position, and fell back to the foot of the hill and threw up temporary works until they were defensible." E. Evans, *O.R.* 36(1) 961-962.

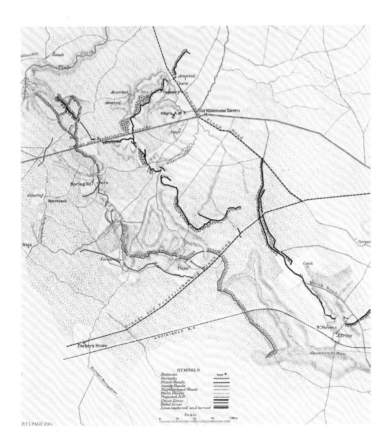

Map of the Wilderness, Virginia, with blue representing Union lines and red, Confederate. Cowles, Davis, Kirkley, Perry. *War Department Atlas*, pl. LV. David Rumsey Map Collection.

May 15—Lay under the fire of rebel sharp shooters. It rained some today.

May 16—Was sick & went to the rear where the cooks were stationed. No fighting since the 12th.

May 17—A cool pleasant day. A battle took place today. Our Regt. were not engaged. I think we rather got the worse of it.

May 18—Was sick still today. No fighting. Warm day.

May 19—Marched about three miles to the left of our line. Drew rations. Was sick all day. Built breast works most all night.

May 20—Lay behind our breast works all day. Had a sharp fight this evening. They attacked us & were repulsed. Was sick all day and ate nothing. A hot day.

May 21—Po River. The army commenced moving this evening. Was sick to day and ate nothing. Hot & pleasant.

May 22—The 9th Corps moved this morning. I started

The 109th lost 104 men from May 7-15 in the Battles of Ny River and Spotsylvania, according to the *Adjutant General's Office Annual Report for the Civil War*, New York, 1910.

The Army of the Potomac - A Sharp Shooter on Picket Duty, 1862. Winslow Homer. *Harper's Weekly*, November 15, 1862.

with the sick but could'nt keep up. Meet some more fellows about a mile & we stoped to a house & got some cake which made me a little stronger. We then went about four miles farther, stoped for the night. Went to a negro womans & got some hoe cake and nice meat. Sleept all night in a shed of straw. A very nice country.

May 23—Started this morning at seven with the sun beating down hot. Went about 6 miles. I stoped for the night at an old planters. Got some hoe cake and some potatoes that one of the boys brought. We sleept in the yard on the ground. At noon we stoped to a house, got some flour. I got an old Negro woman to cook it. Hot & pleasant. Went one mile beyond Guiney Station.

May 24—Got some rye bread & coffee & started on our march. Clear & hot. Left the other boys about a mile from where we staid all night and marched alone to Milford Station. There found the Cavlry Corps. Got a good supper of the boys. Went with the wagon train about two miles, met one of our regiment going to the Regt. Marched total 11 miles. Took the railroad 9 miles.

May 25—Warm and pleasant. It rained some during the night. Marched 6 miles, camped with one of our boys & wagon train of Cavlry. It rained this evening. Gave $1.75 for a little can of turkey. Picked some ripe strawberries yesterday.

May 26—Marched a little ways & stoped and got something to eat at a negro hut while it rained. Left Goodwin & went to Chesterfield Station. Did'nt know what road to take so staid all night there. Got a quater of pig. A part of the Sixth Corps staid there all night. Marched three miles.

May 27—Marched from Chesterfield Station to within two miles of the Panmunkey River with General Rickles Division Sixth Corps, 6 miles. It is hot and pleasant.

May 28—Warm and pleasant. Crossed the Panmunkey River and went one beyond to 2nd Corps camp four miles. Gave myself up to the provost guard of the 2nd Corps to be

On May 21, having failed to dislodge Lee's troops from Spotsylvania at the cost of 17,500 soldiers to Lee's 10,000, the Army of the Potomac moved southeast toward the North Anna River, again trying to get between the Rebels and Richmond. The 9th Corps, in charge of wagon trains, moved on the 22nd. Mason Whiting Tyler, *Recollections of the Civil War* (New York: G. P. Putnam's Sons, 1912) 163. By this time, John was too sick to move with his company and proceeded on his own. He foraged rations and several times got "hoecake," thin bread made with corn meal, water, and salt, baked by black women. As John was walking and hitching rides on wagons and trains attempting to catch up with his unit, the Army of the Potomac reached the North Anna's north shore on May 23 and again found Lee's troops waiting. On the 25th, Grant tried to pierce the Confederate line, but was forced to withdraw. John caught up with his comrades on June 1 and reported shelling and battles upon his arrival.

taken to my Regt within seventeen miles of Richmond.

May 29—Clear and pleasant. Was taken to general headquarters about 1 1/2 miles & put under guard with Rebel prisoners till night when the Rebs were taken away. Nothing to eat but a little meal, water & salt given to me. Wrote one letter to Harriet.

May 30—Was taken two miles to Grants Headquarters then sent to the 9th Corps Headquarters two miles more. Staid all night. had nothing to eat but a little peice of beef, half cup of coffee & two crackers for supper. Nothing for breakfast or dinner.

May 31—Hot & clear. Went to my Regt. They thought I had been taken prisoner. The Regt advanced about a mile to day. Staid to the rear to day. 1 1/2 days rations. Capt. Gorman was killed this afternoon. Had two letters come but they were destroyed.

June 1—Clear and warm. Went to my company this afternoon. Built breast works. Drew three days rations to day. Shells were fired by the rebs & tore things up considerable.

June 2—Came out of the woods back to our iner breast works. Marched about 2 miles. I built breast works through a drenching rain. Supported a battery—it was almost defening! The Rebels flanked us & we had to fall back. It rained during the night.

June 3—Advanced at 5 oclock & drove the Rebel pickets in & occupied the works we lost last night. The Rebels threw shells & bullets at us all day. They wounded 8 or ten of our Regt. We had an order to charge, but it was countermanded. We left at dark & went to the rear & staid all night.

June 4—Warm & pleasant this morning. Lay till two oclock then went to the left about three miles, camped all night in the 2nd line of works. Drawed five days full rations. 1 1/2 days rations of pork. Rained a little in the night.

June 5—Slight drizling rain during the morning. Had wartle berries styed for dinner. They had a fight on our left to

Lee's 59,000 men covered the entire line from the Totopotomy Creek to the Chickahominy, six miles long, with strong earthworks. Behind Lee's line, Richmond was six miles to the west down Old Church Road. But Grant's troops were disoriented and weary. He postponed his attack until June. The Battle of Cold Harbor was a costly failure for the men in blue. An estimated 7,000 of 50,000 Union soldiers were killed in the first few minutes of a mass frontal attack against a three-mile segment of the dug-in Confederate infantry and artillery, compared to about 1,500 Rebel deaths of the defender's 30,000 troops. The 9th Corps lost about 2,000 men at Cold Harbor, where total Union losses were counted at 12,737 Tyler, *Recollections*, 213. A ceasefire went into effect on the 5th to bring in the wounded and dead from between the lines. Many wounded died of exposure after the fight on June 3.

night with success on our side.
Quite a cool day.

June 6—It is a very hot sun
sunny day. Was detailed to
work on a fort. Was relieved
tonight.

June 7—Lay till 1 oclock
at night then moved into
the woods quarter of a mile
to support pickets. Cool &
pleasant. Some of our skirmish
line were taken prisoners. Staid
all night & built breast works.
Hiram Cole was wounded
in the ankle and Corporal
[Chauncy M.] Pomeroy was
killed. The shells flew quite
fast today.

June 8—Lay till one oclock at night then the pickets
begun to fire & we went to the front works till most morning,
then moved back. Drew 2 days rations. Cool, cloudy. Our
army is building two forts & other strong works waiting for
Seige guns. I wrote a letter to day.

"Supported a battery—it
was almost defening!"
John's diary entry, June 2,
1864. Illustration from
Coffin, *Boys of '61,* 318.

June 9—Went out on picket as reserve. Hot and sultry.
Staid all last night and to day. Fort Darling reported taken.

June 10—Drew two days rations this morning. A shell
bursted & wounded D. King & three others in Co. I. Had
a good nights sleep. Cool & windy. Got three letters to day.
Drewed 2 days rations this morning.

June 11—Cool & pleasant. Lay behind the 2nd line of breast
works till night then moved to the front line in front of the fort.
Drew two days rations. Drawed some clothing this afternoon.

June 12—Cool and cloudy. Marched at 8 in the evening
& marched all night to within 3 miles of the White House
Landing. 15 miles.

Military bridge across the Chickahominy River. Photograph by Mathew Brady. Collection of Tioga County Historical Society.

Grant's army moved again, towards the James River. Did Grant intend to attack Richmond from the south side of the James or to continue westward to threaten and perhaps seize Petersburg, site of a railroad confluence, and thus cut Lee's supply lines? Grant was commanding 109,000 Union soldiers compared to Lee's 59,000. But Lee had an excellent defensive fighting force that was hard to dislodge from entrenchments. By June 15, the answer to Grant's destination was clear: it would be Petersburg. No Confederates were seen on the 55-mile march to City Point. Union troops crossed the James from June 15 to 16 on a pontoon bridge. Meanwhile, Lee responded by moving his army towards Richmond. Lee's soldiers also arrived in Petersburg, strengthened old works, threw up new ones, and prepared for battle. On the afternoon of June 16 and throughout the 17th, Winfield Scott Hancock's 2nd Corps and Burnside's 9th Corps

June 13—Stoped till noon then marched 10 miles toward the Chikahominy River. Stoped at 9 & staid until 4 a.m. Cool but dusty.

June 14—Marched at 4, crossed the river at 7 in the morning, then stoped for breakfast. My rations are gone. Marched again at 11, marched until seven, one mile this side [north] of the James River. 15 miles.

June 15—Hot and pleasant. Lay still till night then marched all night. Crossed the James River on Pontoons. Drawed four days rations.

June 16—Marched all day without hardly stoping to eat. Marched to within two miles of Petersburg and lay in the breast works all night. 30 miles. Hot and dusty. Over half of our Regt fell out on the march.

June 17—Today was one of the greatest battles of the war. We advanced at one p.m. through open field of corn, the 2nd & 3rd Brigades following. They throwed grape & shell & cut us all to peices. Only 42 men could be got together after the fight.

June 18—Our Regt advanced again this morning. The Regt charged through the lot and across the railroad & lost 13 men. I was on picket all night.

June 19—The Regt moved back in to the rear to rest. Drew three days rations. I am left in command of the company. Our loss is 130 killed, wounded & prisoners.

pressed troops against Lee's entrenchments with heavy losses. Captain Edwin Evans noted that the 109th New York Volunteers maneuvered most of the night "and participated in the engagement of the 17th, losing quite heavily in killed, wounded, and prisoners" *O.R.* 581. Finally, the Federals overran part of the Rebel defense line. During the night Lee's forces moved to a new and stronger line of fortifications closer to Petersburg. Unable to defeat the Confederates by storm, Grant began the siege of Petersburg, which was to last almost 10 months, until April 2, 1865. Sickness, desertion, battle fatigue, and casualities from sharpshooting and shelling took a heavy toll on both armies. Lee deployed his forces thinly over 35 miles of front, from east of Richmond to southwest of Petersburg. McPherson, *Ordeal by Fire,* 447.

Pontoon bridge on the James River. Johnson, Ridpath, and others, *Campfire and Battlefield,* 364.

Petersburg, V.A.
June 20, 1864

Dear Friend,

It has been a long, long time since I heard from you last
& you cannot imagine how much I want to hear from you.
I should have written to you before now even if you did not
write to me but I could not learn where you were. I was sick
while at Spottsylvania & when they marched from there was
left behind to do the best I could. I bought & begged my
way through the country for ten days before I reached my
company, seven miles of Richmond & for three days through
an enemys country, likely to be taken prisoner at any minute.
Ten of our men were taken not fifty rods from where I was. I
cannot describe to you what I suffered during that ten days!
Sick, tired & hungry, it seemed to me as though I should have
to give up entirely. I would not have run a step to have got
out of the hands of the rebs. While I was away from the Regt
the mail came & they thought I was taken prisoner, so they
destroyed the letters after opening them & finding no money.
One came for me from Speedsville & I did'nt know but what
it might have been from you. I will venture at last to write to
Speedsville & if you should receive it, answer it imedietly and

"I bought and begged my
way through the country
for ten days before I
reached my Company..."
John. Illustration, Johnson,
Ridpath, and others, *Campfire and Battlefield,* 323.

Right, map of the ap-
proaches to Petersburg,
1863, with red represent-
ing Confederate defenses.
Cowles, Davis, Kirkley,
Perry. *War Department Atlas,* pl. XL. David Rumsey
Map Collection.

General Lee tried to lift the siege of Petersburg with a creative strategy. Several Federal defeats in May and June 1864 and a retreat by Union troops into West Virginia left the Potomac unguarded and Washington exposed to attack. Lee sent Lt. General Jubal Early's Army of the Valley, reinforced to 15,000 men, into Virginia's Shenandoah Valley with orders to cross the Potomac and to threaten Washington. Lee hoped Grant would be forced to weaken his army to protect the capital and might be forced to abandon the siege of Petersburg. By July 11, Early was within five miles of the White House. Grant responded to Washington's panic by sending the 6th Corps and other army remnants. The Rebels were ousted. Grant, to prevent further raids from the Shenandoah Valley, ordered the valley devastated. That took time. Early's threat and the ensuing chases and battles as his army retreated provided the desired diversion, but not a lifting of the siege of Petersburg. Early's feint enabled Lee to stock his storehouses as best he could and to reinforce Petersburg's defenses in preparation for a winter siege.

you will receive my everlasting regards. We have'nt but a few men left in our Regiment. In the battles of the Wilderness & Spotsylvania we lost about 300 men & last Friday the 17th we charged across a corn field about 1 P.M. in the afternoon & when we came out all we could get together was 42 men out of 220 men. The next morning the report was made out & we lost one hundred and two men killed, wounded and missing. Our company had one missing, James Phillips & two wounded. Very lucky to the other companys. Our Capt was wounded so I am in Command of the company & it is commanded by a Corporal. Also, there is'nt but one company in the Regt commanded by a commissioned officer; the most of them are sick. Capt Gorman & [Marshall] Warwick is killed & Sergt Jones and Sergt Barton are killed. Sergt Benedict, Capt Evans, Sergt Chandler are wounded. About 400 men have now been lost in the Regiment. Our company only musters 12 effective men. Co. K lost 32 men in the last charge. The grape and canister shells & bullets that pored into our ranks was awful to behold. No words can express or pen portray the awful scene through which we passed. Men falling dead & dieing all around you. We won the victory but it was dearly won. Burnsides whole corps was in the charge & most dreadfully cut up. Our loss was ten to their one if not more. The rebels have strong works in front of us this side of Petersburg, this side of the city near the railroad. I dont know but Grant will take Petersburg, but it will be at the sacrifice of a good many men. Gen Grant is bound to massacre the whole Army or take Richmond & it is my opinion that before he takes it the whole army will be sacrificed. Richmond never can be taken. They have good fighting men & a good many of them. I have been very fortunate so far, never have been hit yet, not enough to make a scratch. I dont know how soon I shall fall but I trust I shall live to see the day when war will cease & the people be once more united & we all can return home to our friends & loved ones & enjoy the blessings of

The "line of battle" charge tactic had a chance of success when smoothbore muskets fired round lead balls, which had an effective range of perhaps a hundred yards. If enough men charged quickly, they could sometimes overrun the enemy before their opponents could reload. However, the Civil War used new technology that was much more deadly at a longer range. Muskets with rifling (spiral grooves) inside the barrels imparted a spin that gave bullets more speed and accuracy. And a reconfiguring of the bullet into a pointed cylindrical shape inflicted much more damage when it struck. Effective killing range increased to half a mile. Adams. *Doctors in Blue*, 114; Susan Provost Beller. *Medical Practices in the Civil War* (Cinncinati, Ohio: Betterway Books, 1992) 27-29; Catton, *Short History*, 148).

Letter courtesy of the Berkshire Historian's Office.

John wrote: "The grape, canister shells & bullets that pored into our ranks was awful to behold." Illustration, Johnson, Ridpath, and others, *Campfire and Battlefield,* 112.

peace which we have so long been deprived of. This has been the greatest campaign of the war. For nearly two months we have been marching and fighting. We have marched about two hundred & seventy (270) miles since we left Alexandria. Our company loss is 31 men. I will give you a list of some of the killed - Sergt D. R. Wright, Private Elizer Goodrich, Frank Osburn, James Reese, John King, Joseph Hoyt, Samuel Brumaghim. Wounded—Sergt Edwin Stepson, R.M.G. Akins, Corporal J. M. Parker, George Gates, Charles Wade, Private Frank Quick, Washington Johnson, William French, Jerome Rodney, Samuel Blim, James Payne, Melody, Frank Braily & others. Write soon & I will give you more of the particulars in my next letter. Write a long letter. From your true friend and well wisher.

John Tidd

PS. Please send this, whoever receives it, to the one directed & you will receive my thanks. Direct to the 1st Brigade, 3rd Division, 9th Army Corps. Our battle flag was lost in Spotsylvania and the state flag was shot into in the charge the other day.

John previously had written several times that he wished to be present to help capture Richmond. Now he was nearly there. The fall of Petersburg would be a prelude to the capture of Richmond. He had witnessed and experienced an unimaginable and devastating reality of war getting there. He was at the heart of the action. However, his letter spoke more eloquently of hoping to live so he could return home than of the glories and patriotism of war and victory. Increasingly, his letters and diary entries had become full of despair. Those who had escaped death and serious wounds were plagued by illnesses, hunger, exhaustion, and harsh living conditions, punctuated by long marches from one battle site to the next. Depressed, hungry, many with untreated wounds, they continued to follow orders.

Near Petersburg
August 8th 1864

Dear Friend Amelia,

Once more I take the pleasure of writing you a few lines to inform you that I am still alive & well as could be expected. I am excused from duty by the Dr. & have been since the fight. I am not very sick. My apetite is poor & the Dr. says I am threatened with feaver. Very near half of the Regt are unfit for duty. Have only about 65 for duty. It is very sickly this month. The weather is very hot with not much of any air stirring & besides the water is very poor in some places. Oh! If I were with you to day I know you would give me something I could eat. I think it would make me well to see

In early June, Henry Pleasants, colonel of the 48th Pennsylvania, persuaded high command to allow his unit to try to place a mine under a portion of the Confederate line at Petersburg. His men, many of whom were coal miners, accomplished the feat. On the morning of July 30, four tons of powder exploded, leaving a 500-yard gap in the center of Lee's Confederate lines. An assaulting Union column rushed forward. Planning had not considered adequately the possibility that the onrushing men would be stalled or trapped in the crater. The Confederates, rallying from their surprise and confusion, concentrated around the rim from every side. Lee's artillery zeroed in on the crater. The Rebels poured shot and shell upon the unfortunate men trapped within the maze of the demolished fort. The Federals' attempt to charge through the Confederate line was prevented by the crater, and their efforts ended in failure. Illustration, Johnson, Ridpath, and others, *Campfire and Battlefield*, 400.

Aftermath, Battle of the Crater, Petersburg, Virginia. Photograph by Mathew Brady. Collection of Tioga County Historical Society.

John's diary entry, July 30, 1864: "The fort was blew up in our front and we charged up to the fort and lay there most all day when we were defeated and driven back to our own works. The rebs captured about 2,000 prisoners, killed and wounded. We lost 55 in our regiment. Colonel Catlin lost a leg. Colonel Stilson was wounded. Five of our company was lost. Was relieved tonight."

The 9th Corps was accused of botching the Battle of the Crater and ruining the best chance to penetrate the Confederate breastworks at Petersburg. General George Meade was particularly critical of General Ambrose E. Burnside's leadership failures in this instance. Burnside's military career was effectively finished. He went on leave shortly thereafter and never returned to military duty, resigning his commission in 1865. Catton, *Short History*, 200; Grady McWhiney. *Battle in the Wilderness: Grant Meets Lee* (Fort Worth, Texas: Ryan Place Publishers, Inc., 1985) 80.

you awhile without takeing any thing. We are on the picket line again—came here on Saturday last. There is as much picket fireing as usual, dont you beleive. I have run a narrow chance of my life since commencing this letter. Three shells from our own batteries bursted & the peices flew all around me so that I spilt a bottle of ink which is worth more than the whole Southern Confederacy.

Our Corps, the 30th of July, is five thousand six hundred (5,642) and forty two. Did'nt I guess pretty well? You know I put it at six thousand. The rebels are trying Gen Grants plan now—undermineing. They blowed up a picket post the other day; killed one man and wounded some more. They undermined one of our forts, but we found it out & removed the guns back. It is now reported that they are undermineing our picket line where our Regt are & they are diging to stop them if possible. It has got to a great pass, trying to blow one another up, bury them alive, but our great Stregetic Grant commenced it, as they call him. A warfare fit only for uncivilized nations & the present Administration.

A good deal is said about who was to blame in the fight of Saturday. Some says Gen Mead, others Burnside, c & c . It is my opinion that if any Gen is to blame, it is no one but Gen Grant himself. He stood right where he could see every thing with Mead & Burnside by his side. If things were not going right, why did he not order it differant. Why was McClellan

John basically was correct. Meade was commander only in name. Lt. General Grant issued the important orders.

called a traitor because he failed to take Richmond with one half, yes, one third the Army Grant has had? Grant has lost more men then McClellan has. It is one complete graveyard through this country. You can see where they have been buried most every where. You cannot imagine what a feeling there is against the Administration & the continuance of the war. The commander of the Regt said he did'nt consider it

City Point, Virginia. Soldiers' graves near General Hospital. c. 1865. Library of Congress, Prints and Photographs.

any disgrace whatever to be dismissed from the service from this Army. They would be glad to get out of it in that way. McClellan is all the go now for the next President.

Two years have passed since I first enlisted in the United States Service. One more long year yet to serve if fortunate enough to live through it, (which God grant that I may), unless it should be settled (the war I mean), which I believe will be if the right President is elected. It seems like a long, long time to be where I cannot see you or hear from you very often. I hope you will answer my letters as fast as they come. I would like to hear from you often. It has now been ten months since I saw you & I presume I shall not have a chance to get home under one year longer. What do you think about my enlisting over again this fall? They say we have that chance in a few days. Would you like to have me serve three years longer? If you say no, I say no too. But, if you say yes, I wont promise you that. Yes is a hard word to say. I have'nt heard from Frank or Helen in a long time. Since the boys got pay the most of them have been gambling it away night & day. Some have lost every cent they got. Others have been drunk a number of times. I am glad I never do so. I never played for any thing in my life nor never will. I never have been drunk & I trust never shall. I have seen enough of it. I would not use it for nothing else, only for your sake; but because I think it a dangerous habit & wrong. It must be much pleasure to be so near home. Tell me all the news in Speedsville & give my respects to Mrs. Reed and all inquiring friends.

John Tidd

PS: I forgot to tell you that we have a new kind of grey back down here...body lice. (Now dont you laugh!) I would like to have you tell me what the L in your name stood for. I never knew.

John may not have been entirely tongue-in-cheek with his musing about re-enlisting. There were powerful incentives. Volunteers were tempted by bounties that could be as high as $1,000 and the status of being "veteran volunteers" Catton, *Short History*, 209.

Three miles from Petersburg
August 31st [1864]

Friend Amelia,

I received your most welcome letter last Sunday. I have not had time to answer it till to day & would'nt now, but am excused from duty. The way we have been used has used me up & a good many more. The 19th of August we left Petersburg and came to the Yellow House on the Weldon Railroad, about five miles from Petersburg where the 5th Corps had the fight the day before. About 2 P.M. the rebels attacked the 5th Corps & our Corps advanced in line of battle through the swamps and into the wood. The loss in our Regt was 8 killed, 9 wounded and a few missing, in all about 25. Our Company had two killed & one supposed to be wounded & sent off to the 5th Corps. Now all the track we have of him is one of that Corps described such a man who belonged to the 109th. You know him—it was Erastus Benton, the one that staid in Reeds kitchen so much the night before going to Binghamton. I did'nt go into the battle nor did'nt intend to; it has played out, this fighting. I never will shoot another reb, only to save my own life. I consider it nothing but murder.

Last Thursday the 2nd Corps had a fight five or six miles to the left. We went there to support them but got there too late to help. The rebels broke through the 2nd Corps, took their breastworks, captured 13 pieces of artillery & took a good many prisoners. They run, threw their arms away & every thing.

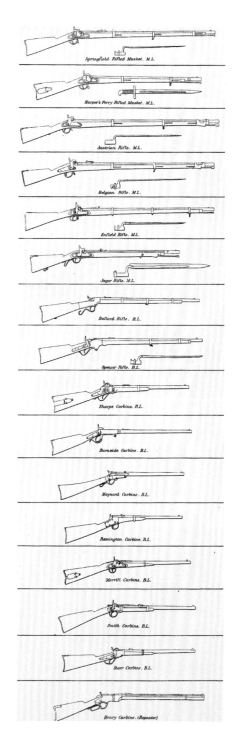

Some had no hat or cap on. It was nothing but a mob, a Bull Run affair. One half never had a gun. Our Corps was then ordered back where they started from and came back in the night. I layed right down beside the road in the edge of the woods & staid all night. The most of our company doing the same, expecting every minute when the rebs would be on us, which would suit me first rate—would fare better than here. Saturday we came here, two miles to the right of the Yellow House, where we have been building breastworks and fixing up camp ever since. Some think we will stay here a month or two. I am very anxious to hear from the Chicago Convention to who is nominated, but it dont make much differance who is the candidate for President to me. I shall vote, if I live, for any one they nominate, if it is Vallandingham.

Elson is in Owego to work. How I wish I was to home. I would give all I have to be free now. My respects to all and write soon. From your friend,

John Tidd

"...a Bull Run affair," refers to a battle in which the Union soldiers threw down their arms and fled. Confederate soldiers collected and used the Union weapons. Left and below: Weaponry. Cowles, Davis, Kirkley, Perry. *War Department Atlas*, pl. CLXXIII. David Rumsey Map Collection.

Clement L. Vallandigham was a controversial Ohio congressman and nationally known Peace Democrat.

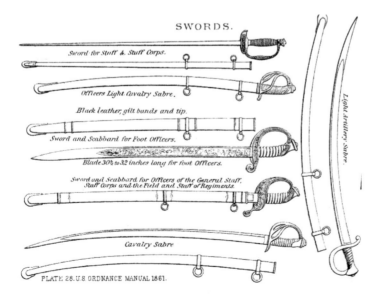

SWORDS.

Sword for Staff & Staff Corps.

Officers Light Cavalry Sabre.

Black leather, gilt bands and tip.

Sword and Scabbard for Foot Officers.

Blade 30% to 32 inches long for foot Officers.

Sword and Scabbard for Officers of the General Staff, Staff Corps and the Field and Staff of Regiments.

Cavalry Sabre

Light Artillery Sabre.

PLATE 28. U.S. ORDNANCE MANUAL 1861.

John describes his unit's role in seizing the Weldon Railroad on August 18 and 19, 1864. By threatening Richmond on the north, Grant forced Lee to move troops from Petersburg. This presented an opportunity to capture Weldon Railroad, which was exploited. Union lines were permanently advanced to this point.

Letter courtesy of the Berkshire Historian's Office.

September 5th 1864

Dear Friend,

It is with pleasure that I received & perused your letter and with much pleasure will answer it. We are still living where we were the last time I wrote you & hope we will stay here all the fall. We have lots of fatigue duty to. We have to be up about one half of the time nights and then every one of us have to get up at half past three or four oclock in the morning. The weather is getting quite cool, nights especilly. Our rations consists of nothing but hard tack, coffee and a little bacon. Hardtacks are full of worms. I dont know how long it will be before we will have another fight; it may be in a week and may not be in two months. I hope I can get a furlough this fall or winter; but dont expect it.

There is great talk of our Regt going back on the Washington & Baltimore Railroad. Col. Catlin is in Washington with his friends doing their best to get us back. Catlin says he will have us there; his one leg will have a great influence. And Gen Martindale said the other day that we were going to have our winter quarters on the Baltimore & Ohio Railroad. It's too good to be true. I dont think myself there is any need of worrying about my reenlisting. I would not enlist for all the green backs Uncle Sam has got. No, I will not be provoked at you for telling me what you heard of my swearing; but I should like to know who told such stories about me. I wish you would tell me. As for the truth of the report—is all a lie. I have never uttered an oath since I have been in the Army nor never intend to. I never can remember of swearing but twice in my life & that was years ago. Whoever tells any such stuff, you can tell them they lie to their faces. I am Corporal no more, I gave up the office, had rather be a Private. Am better off here in the field. Oh, how I wish I was up there to get some of them harvest apples. All we can get here is hazz apples, three cents apiece. Peaches

Letter courtesy of the U.S. Army Heritage and Education Center, Carlisle, Pennsylvania, part of the Winey Collection.

John has been modest about his military rank. The Company Descriptive Book shows he was promoted to 8th corporal in October, 1862 and to 7th corporal in November. He held that rank until September 1, 1864, when due to illness he was reduced to the ranks as a private.

we dont have any. If we were in Maryland we could get plenty of them. I had not heard of Old Blues being sold before. It must have been a great loss to the ladies. We cannot take any more swift rides to Dryden and back. What does Reed do for a liveing? Nothing as usual. I have'nt heard from Helen or Frank in a long time. Have you? We are on our last year—can count the months instead of years. A little over eleven months longer & I am free once more. Wont that be a happy day. Give my respects to all inquiring friends & write soon. You have done well lately. Your friend,

John Tidd

Behind the breastworks, Siege of Petersburg, Virginia. "... A sharp fire was kept up between the Ninth Corps and the Confederates. Everyday from thirty to fifty men were killed or wounded by the sharp-shooters or by shells from the mortars. The casualties were equally great on the Confederate side." Coffin, *Redeeming the Republic*, 366-67.

September 18, 1864

Friend Amelia,

I received your ever welcome letter this morning. I dont
know as I shall answer it to day, but will commence it at least.
It is a cloudy day & looks like rain. It has been quite dry of
late—not haveing rained any since the last of August. We
have been on fatigue duty the most of the time strengthening
our works. They are the strongest I have ever seen. We are in
a pretty good place, no picket fireing. The rebel pickets in our
front, are half or three quarters of a mile from ours. Ours are
in the woods. On the right of us is the Secont Corps. There
is picket fireing night & day. I should'nt wonder if we staid
here a month or two. A staff officer says we will stay here that
length of time. I hope so at least.

September 21st

At last I have set down to fnnish this letter. I have nothing
much to write—no news of importance but what you no
dought, ere this, have heard through the news papers. I
dont think there is any chance of our leaving here this
winter. I should'nt wonder if Lincoln was elected again on
account of the power of the Administration. All the power

Fatigue duty consisted
of work such as building
entrenchments and breast-
works. Above, defensive
positions of Fort Sedgwick,
near Petersburg, Virginia.
Timothy H. O'Sullivan,
1865. Library of Congress,
Prints and Photographs.

of the Government will be used to elect him by fair or by foul means. They are now distributing political documents throughout the army and not allowing Democratic papers or other documents in the army unless sent through the mail to private soldiers. They are not allowed to be circulated through the camps. Not a Democratic paper have I seen in the army except in the way spoken of. There are more Little Mac men in this Regt at present then Lincoln. I shall vote for him if I live if there is not another one in the army. Little Mac forever. Every thing continues quiet—as usual. Picket fireing has ceased.

I would like some of your harvest apples. It seems as if they would taste better than they used to. You wanted to know how I got out of the last fight. Just as easy as could be. When the Brigade advanced, I just stoped & let them go on; easy enough was'nt it? Col Catlin is in Washington. He has lost one of his leggs. I dont think he will ever come in the field again. Maj George W. Dunn is in command of the Regt. Tommy Youngs was taken sick at Cold Harbor & went to Washington & has'nt been back since. I have seen Macs letter of acceptance & like it very well. Owego papers we get now and then, not very often. I would like first rate to have some blackberries and milk but I dont know as I ever shall have that privilige again. Life is uncertain & very uncertain in this country. If not by bullets, by disease. The crowd that collects around the Dr. quarters every morning looks like gatherings at country shows or ball plays. I have known 95 men to be excused from duty in our Regt. Some are excused from all duty & others one half duty—I am now excused from all duty. Have a coff and last night had a night sweat. Not many die here—they are sent of to the Hospital when they get so they cannot hardly get around. I cannot think of any more to write now so good bye.

From,

John

October 13th 1864
Near the Yellow Tavern

Letter courtesy of the U.S. Army Heritage and Education Center, Carlisle, Pennsylvania, part of the Winey Collection.

Friend Amelia,

With much pleasure I take this opportunity of writing you a few lines in answer to your ever welcome missive. I am well at the present time & trust these few uninteresting lines will find you enjoying the same blessing. To day I am on picket in the woods, it is pretty nice business. No picket fireing but dont know how soon before there will be. We are now about three miles farther to the left of where we were when I wrote you last, near the left of our Army. I have no idea that we will stay here long. There has got to be another great battle somewhere on the lines this fall. I hope I shall not be in it. We have lived pretty hard for the last two weeks. Had nothing to eat but hardtacks, coffee and salt pork. We are drawing better rations now. How does Little Mac rate in Speedsville? I hope he will run well, for in my opinion he is the only hope of the nation. Lincolns election will cause four years more of war & bloodshed, which will destroy the liberty of this country forever [and] cause civil war throughout the north as well as south, while McClellans

Grand National Union banner. Liberty, Union and Victory. Currier & Ives, c. 1864. Library of Congress, Prints and Photographs.

election as President, with Congress men enough to support him, will once more bring peace & happiness to our distracted and suffering country. The present administration we cannot expect anything from. Have'nt they tryed these four years & they have failed to conquer the south, & why? Because they have adopted the wrong policy; went against the Constitution, destroyed the liberty of the press & freedom of speech. Men have been thrown into prison & kept there for months & for what? Because they loved their country more than the freedom of a few Negros. They have also invaded the right of the states, rights which the Constitution gave to each state. McClellan will get a good many votes. In the Army most every officer in our regiment will go for him. But they keep still about it. They are afraid to say much against Lincoln for fear of consequences.

One of our pickets was shot a little while ago by one of our own men; he says he thought it was a reb. He was put under arrest for it. The weather here is pleasant but has been very cold & windy for a few days past. At the time you wrote it did not rain here, but the day before it rained quite hard all day. It was a very nasty time. Our Regt was near the field of battle, but we [were] lucky enough to get on the picket line so did'nt get into the regular line of battle. Our Regt also took the skirmish line in the advance the other day to find out where the rebels were. We found where they lay & fell back again. Two or three bullets came pretty close to me but escaped from harm. Yes, I was home one year ago. It does seem a long, long time since that time. But if I live, I have not quite as much time longer to stay, only ten months

more. But, oh how long it will seem; every month seems almost an age. I shall look for that picture of yours every time you write. They have had very bad luck in Speedsville lately. They are all dying off and moving away. I am afraid I will not know anybody by the time I return, not even you. Do you think I will? Now write soon as you get time.

From your friend,

John Tidd.

Former General George B. McClellan was the Presidential nominee on the Democratic ticket. Grand National Democratic banner. Peace! Union! and Victory! Currier & Ives, c. 1864. Library of Congress, Prints and Photographs.

Petersburg
December 20, 1864

Mud march. Johnson, Rid-
path, and others, *Campfire
and Battlefield,* 106.

Friend Amelia,

Your letter was gladly received yesterday morning. We are
still at the front of Petersburg. I should not be surprised if we
staid here all winter. We have had an awful time since I wrote
you last. A brigade was made up from our division. Our Regt
& the 37th Wisconsin were taken from our brigade. We were
marched one mile from camp and lay there from Thursday
night till Saturday at two in the afternoon, waiting for orders
to march to the relief of the 5th Corps, who had gone to
the Weldon Railroad on a raid. They tore up 25 miles of the
track. We had to lay on the ground without shelter and it was
awful cold. One night it hailed & snowed all night. Saturday
at two we commenced to march. Marched all night long – 29
miles, the mud & snow most knee deep. A great many fell out
& come up the next day. It was the hardest marching I ever
saw. I stoped five miles this side of where the Regt stoped &

layed down in the woods in the rain until morning. At two on Sunday we were ordered back to camp again. A skeleton of the Regt reached camp at seven at night, but three quarters of them never got there till Monday. Some froze their feet & hands. One of our Regiment never came back; I presume he froze to death. I never suffered so much in my life.

The weather is more warm & pleasant now but we will have to suffer this winter on picket duty. There is no hope of going to Elmira. It is all talk & nothing more. We will never have any more winter quarters than we have now. Gen Grant dont care anything about his men. He is nothing but an old tyrant. I expect to be moving about all winter. Thanksgiving dinner has to pass through to many officers hands before it gets to privates to be much left. I think you would get me up a good meal if I should come home on furlough. Buckwheat cakes would suit me the best of anything. I shall not be home till my time is out. I cannot get a furlough very well, So good-bye for eight months. I would not desert now, under the circumstances. My time is too near out. The most that desert have two or three years to serve & they are much better of down south then here unless they get caught again. There they are free from military life. I should indeed miss Mrs. Reed. I never saw a woman I thought as much of. What part of the West are they going to? Howard Hubbard has not come yet. The pie we got was mince pie. That & apple pie are my favorites. You will have to excuse me for this time for I cannot think of anything more to write about.

Give my love to all. Good bye. Write soon.

John Tidd

Letter courtesy of Berkshire Historian's Office.

The Army of the Potomac had been in continual conflict with Lee's troops for eight months. John is anticipating another eight months on the front lines before his three-year enlistment is complete.

Eternal Peace

The sultry nightmare was in the past. He had been an animal blistered and sweating in the heat and pain of war. He turned now with a lover's thirst to images of tranquil skies, fresh meadows, cool brooks—an existence of soft and eternal peace.

—Stephen Crane, *The Red Badge of Courage*, 1895

The year 1865 was marked by jubilation as the long horror of the Civil War drew to a close, precipitated by Lee's surrender to Grant on April 9. However, the North also bore the tragic event of President Lincoln's assassination on April 14, and, on an individual level, countless personal sorrows. Many soldiers, including John, who had for years longed for home, faced the bittersweet emotions of returning home to a changed world, not always matching what they had envisioned, especially as they themselves continued to be plagued by injury and illness suffered during the war.

Beginning in 1864, John's health deteriorated steadily. His diary and letters mentioned being excused from duty due to illness in early April of 1864. His health problems, undiagnosed, persisted when his regiment was at Spotsylvania, and nagged on through May. John's illness was much more serious by the end of August, when he had "fainted away." He was being excused from duty for longer stretches at a time. He complained of poor appetite. The doctor warned him that he risked fever. His miseries were compounded by occasional battle, serving picket duty, being shelled, the constant physical labor necessary to build breastworks, and the persistent emotional stress of seeing the dead and wounded everywhere.

Soldiers of the 9th Corps soon learned not to expect much medical assistance. It wasn't until the end of May that they even were assigned a medical corps and ambulances of their own. If they survived a wound, there was a reasonable chance

Alfred A. Phillips, Editor, *The Moss Rose, for 1848* (New York: Nafis and Cornish, 1848) cover.

they would be taken prisoner by Confederates before they could be evacuated behind Union lines. Routine sickness often was ignored by their medical personnel, because there were so many men with much worse health problems, as a result of battle wounds.

The 9th Corps left Annapolis before any medical organization could be formed. Transportation shortages meant that

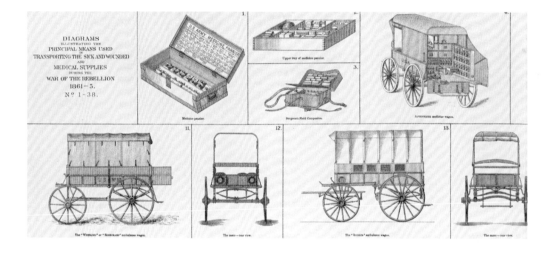

available wagons were allocated to transport of food, ammunition, and other army supplies. A. McParlin, Union surgeon and Director of the Medical Corps for the Army of the Potomac, wrote: "The greater number of the regimental surgeons had drawn a full three months regimental supply at Annapolis, which had to be left behind, and the only medical supplies with the Corps were contained in the hospital knapsacks, in a few medicine chests, and baggage, which were almost always inaccessible and useless, and in 12 Dunton medicine wagons. The ambulance corps was still very imperfect. Many ambulances were broken and badly in need of repair, the greater part of the stretchers were missing, very few had water kegs, and no hospital stores were carried in the ambulance boxes. Citizens had been hired as drivers for the ambulances, but the majority of them had deserted at Fredericksburg, and their places filled by the stretcher-bearers, many of whom seemed to have been selected on account of their worthlessness in other situations."

A. McParlin, *O.R.* V36(1), 240.

John's letter to Amelia of December 20, 1864—after the men had marched and fought their way 270 miles south, fighting at the Wilderness, Spotsylvania, and Cold Harbor (along

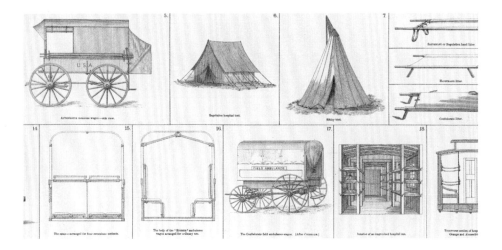

with other skirmishes)—made this grim report: "We are still at the front of Petersburg. I should not be surprised if we staid here all winter. We have had an awful time since I wrote you last."

There was still resilience in his life, however. His first letter of the new year to Amelia, on January 13, 1865, was almost jovial. He was fantasizing about what he might have been up to at Christmas past had he been where Amelia was. And he was up to his old tricks, slyly teasing Amelia.

Left, and above, illustrations of the principal means of transporting the sick and wounded. Cowles, Davis, Kirkley, Perry. *War Department Atlas,* pl. CLXXIV. David Rumsey Map Collection.

Near, Petersburg, VA.
January, 13th 1865

Friend, Amelia
                    Welcomely
was your letter received; & perused it
with much pleasure. It has
been a lone — long time Since I
heard from you last, most a
month, your letter is dated the
3d & mailed the 7th. How is that
It Seems like a long time to wait
for a letter from you. Well
Christmas and New Years have
come and gone, and I Suppose
you have had a good time. I
hope So at least, I wish I had of
been there too, but if the Lord is willing
another new year will find me
there or some other good place. Do you

Near Petersburg, V.A.

January 13th 1865

Friend Amelia,

Welcomily was your letter received & perused with much pleasure. It has been a long time since I heard from you last, most a month. Your letter is dated the 3rd & mailed the 7th. How is that? It seems like a long time to wait for a letter from you. Well, Christmas and New Years have come and gone and I suppose you have had a good time. I hope so at least. I wish I had of been there too, but if the Lord is willing, another newyear will find me there or some other good place. Do you wish to know what I had? Well, I will tell you. For breakfast pork, hardtack & coffee. For dinner pork & beans, and for a change at supper we had pork & coffee, hardtack of course included. Don't you wish you could have as good. My box did'nt get here till the 7th of this month, three weeks on the road. Every thing in it was as nice as when packed in the box. I thank you very much for the things you sent me. They were all very nice, better than I deserve I am sure. I hope I may some time repay you all for remembering a poor lonely soldier some thousand miles away. I shall always keep them in remembrance. The chicken & pies kept firstrate. Nothing was hurt or nothing jamed up. I have had quite a feast out of it. I have plenty of dried fruit left. I was on picket New Years & it was a very cold day. I have been on duty every New Years since I have been out. Yesterday, I was on picket & there was no fireing all day. A flag of truce came in from the rebels in the morning. One of our Officers met them half way between the lines. They sent a sealed envelope to some high Officer, I don't know who, & went back and waited till most night for an answer. It came & they went to their works again. I don't know what it was for there was no fireing during the night or to day. The boys were all up on both sides over the breastworks tradeing for tobacco and chaseing rabbits between the lines. I dont know how long it will last but hope all winter. We have had some very bad stormy weather but now it is quite warm & pleasant again. You had a nice present [for] Christmas. I guess some one must have taken you for a niggar lady or Abolitionist, but are not, are you? They must be mistaken. I think you

think just as much of a white man if he behaves himself, as you do of a nigger. Now realy, dont you? I should try and pay Santa Clause some time in his own coin. What a nice time you must have had at the Christmas tree. I think I could have bettered the choice in pretty girls. I dont know who was there, but there must have been some better looking, Miss Slosson for instance or Miss A. L. Haskell. Now dont get mad for classing you with one so good looking as Miss Slosson for I realy think you good looking or would be if it was not for your homely face. You girls must be almost destitute for beaus. The boys have most all left. It will soon be Valentines Day and I shall look for one sure, seeing I never did have one. I hear Leon Blanchard has got home again. [He] got sick of it soon. I wish I could be with you to day. It would do me more good to see & talk with you awhile then to write a half a dozen letters. I will have to stop now. Be sure & write soon.

   Your most affectionate friend,

                                        John

Christmas on the Rappahannock, near Fredericksburg. The opposing soldiers found ways to communicate and trade with one another in a peaceful manner, as John described in his letter of January 13, 1865. For example, in 1862 the troops traded during Christmas. Pickets launched little sail boats back and forth across the river, bearing coffee, sugar, and pork from the Union side and parched corn, tobacco, and ripe persimmons from the Rebel side. Coffin, *Drum-Beat*, 459-461.

Division Hospital, Feb 17th 1865
Near Petersburg, Virginia

Friend Amelia,

I am in the Division Hospital sick. Came here last Sunday. I have done no duty in a month and never expect to do any more. The Dr. says that I will never get well and I think the same. He sent me here on a disease of the lungs. I am going before the board of examination for a discharge when our head Dr. gets back. He has gone home on a fifteen days furlough. We have corresponded for a long time, but I dont know but what it had better stop now for we cannot be any thing to one another but friends. I shall always remain single. I don't think I shall live a great while & even if I should I shall never get well. You can act your own pleasure about writing letters of friendship. I don't feel like writing any more at present. So good bye.

From your friend,

John Tidd
Co. B. 109th Regt. N.Y.V.

Civil War medicine in the field for the wounded was rudimentary, even when the medical corps had a chance to get established, as it did during the siege of Petersburg. During battle, wounded men who were not ambulatory often bled to death under fire. Their would-be rescuers were stopped by sharpshooters all too many times. Wounded who were lucky enough to be evacuated to the rear found overwhelmed medical personnel often without needed equipment, facilities, and supplies. Two further major causes of death were the lack of ambulances and shortages of doctors. Sick soldiers were lower on the triage priority list. If their conditions became so bad they couldn't perform routine duties for long periods of time, much less engage in battle, they were removed from the front or near-front lines and sent to hospitals. John finally wound up in that situation. On February 17, 1865, he wrote a pivotal letter to Amelia.

5th Ward
N.S.A. Hospital, York, P.A.
March 28th 1865

Friend Amelia;

Your letter was welcomely received the 25th of this month. I have not felt much like writing for the last few days & in fact dont any of the time or I should answer all letters as soon as received because I have nothing else to do. I don't know as I am any better. Keep about the same. Sometimes a little better & sometimes a little worse. The worst of it is what I eat, I cannot keep down. I vomit it all up. Cod liver oil & whiskey is my medicine now with cough medison. I dont know when I shall get a furlough. It is hard work to get one here now. I am trying to get transferred to the Elmira Hospital. The member of Congress from our district is going to try & get me there. If that fails, I will try some other way of getting transferred. My courage is good & I laugh pretty hearty now & then. I guess we did have a thunder storm the same night. I see they are most all going away from Speedsville. I shall not know the place or inhabitants if I should go home. I should have to be carried around if I went around much for I cannot walk but a little ways. I expect our Regt have been in another battle before Petersburg. I am anxous to hear from it. I cannot write any more now, so good bye.

From your friend,

John

John's March 28 letter showed concern for how his regiment fared in the Petersburg battle of March 25. This was General Lee's last desperate counter-punch, led by General John B. Gordon at dawn against the Union stronghold of Fort Stedman, on the Richmond-Petersburg line. Having captured the fort and some Federal trenches, but finally being repulsed and pushed back behind Confederate lines by noon, the Rebels were thwarted in their last desperate attempt to break the siege. It cost them dearly. Some 4,800 to 5,000 casualties were suffered. A few days later, April 2, 1865, the Confederate Petersburg line was at last penetrated by the Federals. Lee ordered some 400 to 600 men from Wilcox's division and Harris's brigade into Fort Gregg with instructions to hold it to the last breath. They were under attack by a full Union division. Hand-to-hand combat took place. When surrounded and their situation hopeless, the Fort Gregg Rebels finally surrendered. They suffered 55 dead and wounded. March 28 was John's last mention of the war in his letters to Amelia. Of course, the war did not last

much longer. Two weeks after the Fort Stedman fight and a week after Fort Gregg's bloody bayonets, Lee surrendered to Grant at Appomattox Court House, Virginia, on April 9, 1865, having fought all the way in his limping retreat from Richmond and Petersburg. It is estimated that from March 29 to April 9, the Confederates lost 6,266 men killed and wounded.

Lee, seated, at his Franklin Street House, Richmond, Virginia, after the war. Mathew Brady, 1865. Collection of Tioga County Historical Society.

N.S.A. Hospital, York, PA
April 6th 1865

Friend Amelia,

I received your welcome letter this morning. I am a little better than when you wrote before. I have been here most seven weeks. I am going to get a furlough pretty soon. It was made out this afternoon. It is a sure thing this time. I will be home about next Thursday. I will come to Speedsville the next week after if able. You will have to excuse me this time. I have been writing home & I am now tired out. So good bye till I see you.

Good night,

John

John was admitted to an army hospital in York, Pennsylvania, arriving on February 21 and remaining there until April 12, when he received a furlough to visit home. After arrival in Elmira, New York, he was honorably discharged on May 26.

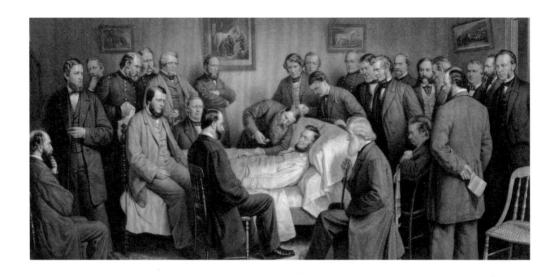

Candor, Tioga Co, N .Y.
May 6th 1865

President Lincoln on his deathbed after being shot by John Wilkes Booth at Ford's Theater, in Washington, on April 14, 1865. Alexander Hay Ritchie, c.1875. Library of Congress, Prints and Photographs.

Friend Amelia;

With pleasure I take pen in hand this morning to write you a few lines to let you know how I am getting along. I am a little better I think. I have got my furlough extended twenty (20) days. Am going to Ithaca to Doctor with Dr. Bishop next Monday. I have not been to Mr. Bushs yet. I dont know as I shall before I go back to the hospital. They are giveing all soldiers in hospitals their discharges. I have been to Mr. Blewers. They are not keeping school this summer. He is keeping meat market. You will find them photographs I spoke to you about in this letter. When I get some good ones taken, I will send you one of them.

Please write to me as soon as you can. Direct to Ithaca.

Please excuse this short letter and I will try & do better next time. My respects to your mother.

From your true friend,

John

Ithaca, May 18th 1865

Friend Amelia;

I am a great deal better than when I first came to Ithaca. Am gaining every day. Dr. Bishop thinks I will get along if I am careful. I walked to Fall Creek yesterday to a caravan, one & a half miles. I wish you had been here to go. There was all kinds of animals. I am going to Elmira next Monday if nothing happens. I dont have to go any further than there. They will send for my descriptive list & muster me out in Elmira. They will give me eight or ten days longer furlough so they can have time to make out my papers. I have had one dozzen photographs taken. I guess they are very good. I will send you one in this letter. I hope it will suit you. I picked out the best one. Oh, how I wish I could be with you to day. It is so lonesome, it being a rainy day. The hours pass so quickly away when I am with you. I hope I will be better when I come to see you again than when I was there before. I will come as soon as I can. I may get my discharge first. If so, it will be about the first of June. I am not afraid you will make me sick, but better if anything. You would not do such a thing would you? Yes, I went to Owego Saturday and went home that night.

I should think it would be quite an inducement for me not to be called copperhead, but should hate to trust you. I expect you will call me that hard name the first thing. Then how mad I should be. Mad enough to eat you up with kisses. I am staying with my sister. There is no news to write so I will have to close. You will not have time to write a letter to me before I go away so you may direct it to Candor.

Your friend,

John

The anti-war Democrats were called "Copperheads" because they cut the Indian heads from copper pennies and wore them in their lapels. Catton, *Short History*, 211. John had Copperhead sentiments prior to the election and expressed anti-Lincoln feelings from time to time by 1864.

Candor, June 27, 1865

Amelia,

I am no better and dont know as I ever will be. I did'nt
go to see that Dr. in Ithaca. I found out he was nothing but
a humbug. I am going to Owego to morrow to see a Dr.
White who is comeing there Thursday. He comes there once
in two months. He is reccommended very highly. I shall try
him any way. If he dont cure me, I will try some one else.
If I cannot get well I may as well be dead, as to live, for I
am in misery all the time as it is now. I hope you will have
a good time the Fourth of July. I shall stay home. I would
like to go somewhere, but I dont feel like going any where.
I have applied for a pension & was examined by a Pension
Surgeon. The papers are all made out & I expect are sent to
Washington before this time. There is no trouble in getting it.

I did not get in Ithaca until Monday night so of course did
not see you. Dr. Bishop told me he saw you. We have had lots
of strawberries here this year.

I did not know as you were comeing back to see me again
and I wanted to get back to Speedsville so I could take the
stage.

Believe me to be as ever your friend,

John

Candor, July 21st 1865

Friend Amelia,

I was happy to hear from you. It is quite a while since you
wrote to me. I have been down to Ithaca three or four days
with my youngest sister from Belmont, Alleghany County.
She is going back home next Monday or Wednesday the 24th
or 26th. Then I shall come up to Speedsville in the stage. I
am going to stay there about two week's. Come down and
see me. You can see me at Mr. Reeves. I thought I improved
very much for a few days after I commenced to Dr with Dr.
White, but I dont seem to gain much now. I staid to home
the 4th. Had chicken potpie & lemonade. I saw Helen &
Frank Bush yesterday. I hope George Nixon will find the
theif. I wonder who it can be. You must excuse me this time
for not writing more. I cannot think of any thing to write this
afternoon. I hope I will see you long enough to make it all up.

From your dear friend,

John

Candor, August 17th

Friend Amelia,

I received your letter to day and was very glad to get your photograph. I like it ever so much. It is the best one I have seen of you. It looks more like you. Better looking than the one I have got. I would not part with this for a good deal.

I was in Speedsville one week. I did'nt expect to go away under a week, but I had a chance to ride down to Ithaca but could not ride back. I had business I wanted to attend to as soon as possible, so I went & took the cars home.

I have been very sick since I saw Mr. Owens in Candor. That was Wednesday forenoon. I went home & such pain as I was in the rest of that week (last week) I hope no mortal will ever have to endure. The Dr. was here but did'nt stop the pain. It stoped Monday. Such misery as I was in was almost impossible to bear. I did'nt eat nor drink much of any thing & only weigh about 115 pounds. I am better now but I dont beleive I shall live long. I do not gain any. I rather lose. When fall & winter comes I will gradualy fail till death comes & takes me away. Oh, how much I would like to live, to live for you. I hate to leave you but, I cannot live. But I hope I shall meet you in that upper & better world where sorrow & sickness never comes. I will come and see you if I get able to come to Speedsville again.

Yes, I had a very good visit but we could not injoy it much because she was sick & my self to.

I cannot write more now. Write soon,

John

All subsequent letters looked inward. Like the elderly in their last months, John had lost friends and was isolated from social interactions. He faced an uncertain future. Death was a real possibility, which he did not deny. He suffered from reduced mobility. Under such conditions, almost anyone would lose concern for the doings of the external world and its social, economic, and political issues. His letters increasing make reference to his poor health and infirmities and to the medical personnel to whom he has desperately turned for help. He admits he has lost interest in writing and his letters become terse, unlike his earlier chatty missives. The preservation of life had become his battle, his personal war. He fought like General Lee had fought on the way to Appomattox, defensively without much prospect or hope of gain. He was just barely hanging on. Amelia was on his mind incessantly. He wanted very much to see her again, one last time.

Candor, Sept. 10th / 65

Amelia,

I have got so that it is hard work for me to write. I have been miserable for a long time. Feel a little better now. I dont go no where, have not been able. I was to Owego two weeks ago, but it was to hard a journey for me. Camp Meeting is most over. I have not been yet. If I am able, I shall go the fair to Owego the 2nd & 3rd day. If you go, I may see you there and if I get a good chance, will ride up to your house if you want I should. My side aches so much that I will have to close.

Write soon,

John

Home, Sept 26th

Amelia,

I got your letter the other day. Thought I would come &
see you before I wrote again, but I was taken very sick night
before last and have keept my bed ever since. I am writing
this lieing abed. I was taken with faintness & it was much
as they could do to keep me from fainting away till I got
to vomiting. Mr. Dixon came to see me this morning. He
thought he could help me but I dont know. I dont know
when I shall come, but as soon as I get able.

Oh, I would like to see you once more but I don't know
as I ever shall be able. I shall have to stop so good bye. Write
soon.

John

Home, Oct. 6th

Dear Friend,

I am now upon a bed of sickness which I never expect
to leave more then a few minutes to a time. Oh, I want to
see you before I die. If you want to see me liveing, you must
come before long. You _must_ come, I may not live till you get
this letter.

Come right away. Good bye. I am tired out.

John

Home, October 13, 1865

Dear Friend Amelia,

I am very sick and dont expect to live but two or three days. I am sick a bed and dont leave my bed to have it made up. I have watchers every night and day. I dont eat any thing but drink a little porage and water. Be shure and come without fail if you want to see me alive as soon as you git the letter.

Pam writing for John Eliza Tidd

John Eliza Tidd died on October 17, 1865. The identity of Pam, who helped John write his last letter, remains unknown.

Epilogue

In the hustle and bustle of daily life 150 years after the Civil War, it is sometimes easy to forget that the people who lived and fought the war were not all that unlike us. They were human, not marble statues in front of our county courthouses. We commemorate them with monuments, but the extent and the nature of their sacrifices dim over time. The story that John Tidd lived and recorded for Amelia helps bring their lives and the Civil War era to life for contemporary readers. The quotidian facts of their sacrifices, longings, perceptions, and feelings remain the life blood of history.

John's sister, Minerva, wrote a letter to Amelia on November 12, 1865, a month after his death:

> *Friend Amelia,*
>
> *You wanted to know what John said a bout your going a way that morning. He did not say any thing, any more than he did when you was here. He did not talk a bout any thing. He new every boody till the last. He was ask if he thought he was deying. He said he did not no. He died very easey. When I got back that day and went in the room, I see he would not live long. He died the nex day 3 in the after noon.*
>
> *I sspose you have got that diary by this time. We sent it to you. I shal have to close fore my pen is so poor. I shoud like to hear from you now and then if you fel so dispose to writ.*
>
> *Minerva Cooper*

We infer from Minerva's letter that just before John's death Amelia made a final visit to see him, as he had requested, and that he was conscious on that occasion. Minerva's letter seems to be a response to an earlier letter from Amelia concerning what John might have said about her visit after she had left

Civil War monument in front of the Tioga County Courthouse. Owego, New York, 2010.

him. Minerva's response indicates that John was responding to questions on his deathbed, but that he hadn't added anything new concerning Amelia's visit. The fact that Amelia cared about what he might have said about her indicates that she also cared about his feelings toward her, although she no longer was certain what his emotions might have been. We can take a measure of satisfaction in her willingness to make the journey to visit him and we also can believe that she, at a minimum, felt deeply enough about him to grant his last wish, knowing as John did that he was dying. It must have been a difficult time for both.

There are about 50 letters written by others to Amelia after John's death that she saved and stored with John's letters.

The one-room school house that Amelia attended in Jenksville. Photographed in 2010.

They give no hint of Amelia's reaction to John's death or answers to our questions about their relationship. Amelia's family letters discuss ordinary lives: who was married, who was sick, who died, what the weather was like, what special events took place for holidays, how the farm animals were doing, and so on. Amelia was still being accused of being slow to write letters, that she was often thought of, that her sisters and brothers and their families and friends had the usual mixture of problems and triumphs. But because we do not have her response to John's letters or any other letter for that matter, Amelia remains somewhat mysterious.

Amelia also wrote to other soldiers with whom she was acquainted, but apparently only kept John's letters and picture. At the time of John's death, Amelia was working as a live-in maid in the home of George and Janette Williams in Rawson Hollow, a position she had held since her 18th birthday. George and Janette Williams divorced around 1871-1872 and Amelia moved out of the Williamses' home and returned to live with her parents in Jenksville, approximately three miles away. She continued to work for George Williams on a commuting basis.

Amelia corresponded with and was courted by at least two suitors after John's death. In 1874, nine years after John's death, she married her employer, George Williams. They had four children: Myra, born in 1876; Clara May, born in 1880; Frank, born in 1881; and Samantha, born in 1885. George Williams died in 1912. Amelia died in 1917.

We can only speculate as to who hid the cache of John's letters and photograph in her daughter Clara's home, in Slaterville Springs. Perhaps Amelia also had lived there with her daughter. If so, it is possible that Amelia hid the letters and other ephemera in the secret compartment.

The view of apple trees in bloom, as seen through the wavy glass at the Jenksville school, is much the same as it was when Amelia was a student nearly 160 years ago.

As for Rawson Hollow and Speedsville today, the rolling hills and creeks would still be familiar to John and Amelia. Amelia would have no trouble recognizing the red one-room schoolhouse, in Jenksville, that she attended in the 1850s. The view of apple trees in blossom seen through the schoolhouse's wavy window panes may be something Amelia once enjoyed. In Rawson Hollow, the original building that housed the inn still stands as a private residence, maintained much as it was in the 1800s. John and Amelia would recognize it immediately. In Speedsville, the residents still gather to enjoy a community barbecue and to hear a band play in the town square.

Speedsville flourished after the Civil War with its triweekly stage to Owego. In 1879, it had a population of 200, two general stores, and a milliner, tailor, wagon shop, gristmill, sawmill, cheese-box factory, hotel, two blacksmiths, three churches, a Masonic Lodge, and a Good Templar Lodge. Industries made bricks, cheese vats, milk cans, and coolers. There was a homeopathic physician and a carriage maker. The Cornet Band gave concerts in the park. Two creamery and cheese factories were started, one in 1879 and the other in 1894. Speedsville went into a decline when river commerce gave way to railroads, and local farmers left the Caroline hills. In 1888 the Speedsville hotel and barn burned, followed by two stores, a barn, and the meat market in 1902. In 1928, a store facing the commons burned.

Present-day Speedsville is no longer self-sufficient. Gone are the mills, shops, stores, and factories that once made the community a kingdom unto itself. The population remains stable. But much of the Speedsville of yore remains only in spirit. Speedsville boasts many of the same surnames as before, with many third- and fourth-generation families living there. The automobile, television, internet, school busing, and other modern technologies and practices have opened the way for much more contact with the outside world. In some ways, Speedsville is a bedroom community now, with residents commuting to Owego, Binghamton, Ithaca, and other places for jobs. Others have found its rolling hills and creeks an attractive place in which to retire or to visit as a

The former Rawson Hollow Inn as it appeared in 2010.

The Speedsville Park often features local bands such as "The Kinfolk." Photographed June 2010.

place for vacation homes. Present day residents may still feel some of the sentiments that Helen L. Bush expressed in a letter to Amelia, dated May 3, 1868.

You wanted to know if I liked Dryden as well as Speedsville. Of course not! What a question! Do you suppose that we could ever like any place better than Speedsville, where there are so many associations collected, such as being helped over the fence on a Sunday evening, or taking walks in the middle of April ...

MAP
OF THE
UNITED STATE
OF AMERICA,
SHOWING THE
BOUNDARIES
OF THE
UNION AND CONFEDERATE
GEOGRAPHICAL DIVISION
AND
DEPARTMENTS,
APRIL 9, 1865.

✱ On April 9, 1865, the Army of the Potomac (MEADE) and the
Army of Northern Virginia (LEE) were operating in the
vicinity of Appomattox Court-House, Virginia.

⧣ SHERMAN'S Army was en route from Goldsborough toward
Raleigh N.C., confronted by the Army of Tennessee and
other Forces under JOHNSTON

Afterword

From his letters and diary, we learn that John Tidd did not have a lot of formal schooling, but had a bright, lively interest in his world and in people. Prior to enlisting in the 109th New York Volunteers, he worked in a cooperage factory. John helped make buckets and barrels for everyday use. The factory required workers who had pride in their craftsmanship. He seems to have joined the Union Army in part because he was a firm patriot. Certainly, he believed in the United States and wanted to see it preserved intact. He was among the first to enlist in Company B. There also was the generous bounty (cash incentives) offered to volunteers and he wanted to make sure his aged father was financially secure. Finally, there was the threat of a draft if the recruiters did not meet their quota. However, his primary reason seems to have been patriotism and a strong conviction that the rebellion was wrong and needed to be put down. Initially he saw the Rebels in black-and-white terms. Eventually however, they became more human in his thinking and he no longer wanted to kill. He also became sympathetic to the Peace Democrats and expressed disapproval of Lt. General Grant and President Lincoln prior to the presidential election of 1864, although he vacillated on whether or not he would vote Republican, Lincoln's party.

Going off to Baltimore by train upon enlisting seemed a lark and a huge adventure. However, by December 1862, John's morale had waned. He alluded to the Union Army's recent setbacks and wished he could go into battle. For the time being, guarding railroads and telegraph lines and the comfortable winter quarters the soldiers had constructed seemed worthwhile, but probably boring. He had developed strong solidarity with his fellow soldiers and was proud of his company and regiment. He sounded irked that the soldiers hadn't been paid

Map of the United States of America showing the boundaries of the Union and Confederate geographical divisions and departments, April 9, 1865. Cowles, Davis, Kirkley, Perry. *War Department Atlas,* pl. CLXXIII. David Rumsey Map Collection.

since they had joined as raw recruits. He did not care for a few of his officers. More and more, his description of home began to sound like a paradise far away, one that wouldn't be reached for a long time. Amelia appeared in his imaginings and longings as his future partner.

John had a firm moral foundation. He could count on one hand the number of times he'd used swear words. He prided himself in not gambling or drinking to excess. He attended church. He read books and newspapers. When he got to Washington, he visited the Patent Office to see the historical artifacts on display. His politics tended to waver, but that may be due to his willingness to listen to political arguments and to examine social issues with an open mind. He assured Amelia that he was not consorting with women while he was away. His most notable flaw from a contemporary perspective was his prejudice against blacks, yet he endorsed the Emancipation Proclamation as soon as he learned of it. He attended black church services. However, his views on slavery tended to be more approving than disapproving.

Unlike Henry Fleming, the main character of *The Red Badge of Courage*, John Tidd never doubted his role as a soldier, and we have no evidence that he feared his first battle. The more he saw of death and destruction, the less enamored he became of what was going on in the war. After his unit became part of the 9th Corps, in late April 1864, it saw action in the Battles of the Wilderness, Spotsylvania Court House, Cold Harbor, and the Crater at Petersburg, as well as in lesser skirmishes and assaults at Ny River, Po River, North Anna River, Totopotomoy Creek, the flank march on Petersburg, and actions at Norfolk Railroad, Weldon Railroad, Poplar Spring Church, Pebbles Farm, Boydon Plank Road, and Thatcher's Run (all in Virginia). The 9th Corps participated in the entire siege, assault, and capture of Petersburg, and its flags were the first to fly over the city. John participated in many of these actions until he became too sick for active duty, in mid-January 1865. Before being excused

Right, Civil War monument in front of the Tioga County Courthouse. Owego, New York, 2010.

from duty, he had determined that he henceforth would never kill a Rebel, except in self-defense. His words implied that he had killed in battle. He said that upon reflection he considered it murder. This is in sharp contrast to his October 12, 1862, boast to Amelia that "I will try and kill as many as two or three for you," as if Confederate soldiers were trophy animals. He had been promoted to higher ranks and was briefly in charge of his company in June 1864, but seemed relieved when he was replaced, preferring to be an ordinary soldier.

As John became enmeshed in the brutal reality of war, it is quite clear that he did not have much grasp of war strategy or a big picture of the conflict. Unlike the generals, with their many worries and overall vision of what was going on and (perhaps) what was about to happen, ordinary infantrymen like John merely followed orders and did the best they could. Thus, he drew his rations, marched when told, knowing only that he had to follow the road he was on or the bridge he was told to cross. He suffered from sore feet and a musket that got heavier with every mile. He stopped to eat when told, turned left or right, went up or down hill, and when the day was through, made his bed. Sometimes, he was not even allowed to sleep for long, but was roused at an early hour to begin marching again, where or why he did not know. He faced battle, when it came, making a stand where he was told or charged a foe of unknown strength and conviction when and where he was directed. He was caught in a series of events that he imperfectly understood, sometimes fought for reasons unknown; reasons that were sometimes noble, sometimes stupid. He longed for home, for peace, for an end to the grit and grime and sickness and hunger and endless motion. He appreciated when the weather was pleasant and when he was fed well and allowed to rest. He sometimes hoped that the place where they were was the place where they'd stay for awhile.

He accepted that he very likely could become one of the more than 600,000 men and women who eventually would

The lush, green, rolling hills of Speedsville, New York, 2010.

die as a result of accident, wound, or disease, but he hoped to survive. That above all. He often had little time for reflection, but sometimes he had too much time to think things over. He seemed to prefer good food and good weather best in all of army life. The past was a blur and he was aware that life at home had changed and would not be as it was when he had left, if and when he returned. But he looked forward to a time of safety, of security, of leisure, and yes, of Amelia's company, although we will never know to what degree Amelia reciprocated John's feelings of affection. Too often, there was only the eternal present that could end at any moment. Perhaps he laughed, secretly, when he thought of the story that went around about the officer who rode up to a cowering group of men facing a line of Rebels in the distance and asked what they were hiding from. "Sharpshooters," he was told. "Stand up, you 'fraidy cats,'" the officer said. "Sharpshooters couldn't hit an elephant at this distance." At that moment, a minié ball smashed through his skull and he toppled from his horse, dead before he hit the ground. The lesson drawn from that story was "Beware the elephant hunters. And beware those who taunt and underestimate the enemy."

John's diary documented his increasing health problems in mid-May 1864, and the topic became more frequent during 1865. He wrote of lack of appetite, "fainting away," and being excused from duty because of sickness. He was unable to keep up with his comrades on long marches. By December 12, he was unable to walk a mile. Eventually, in the middle of January 1865, he was no longer able to serve the Union Army at all. He came to a momentous decision during his week's stay at Division Hospital from February 12 to February 19, 1865. He informed Amelia on February 17 that the doctor had told him he had disease of the lungs, writing, "We cannot be anything to one another but friends. I shall always remain single. I don't think I shall live a great while and even if I should I shall never be well again." In all likelihood, he had tuberculosis, or "consumption," as it was called during his era. The lung disease is characterized by fatigue, weakness, fever ("night sweats"), and chest pain. All those symptoms progressively became worse. Unsanitary food and water, dirt and grime, exposure to many different types of diseases, forced marches, the stress of constant battles, and exposure to extreme weather conditions constantly challenged his immune system's defenses.

John finally was released from military service, with an honorable discharge, on May 26, 1865. He returned to upstate New York where he was attended by Dr. Bishop of Ithaca and rallied for a short time. But by June, his health again deteriorated and he changed doctors, seeking help from Dr. White of Owego. From June until his death, on October 17, 1865, he was in continual misery and was cared for by his sister Minerva at her home in Candor. Unlike a sudden death from a cannon ball, a sword or bayonet, or a bullet, he lived with the knowledge he was slowly dying. He also had to live with his difficult decision that he could have no future with Amelia and that he had notified her of that fact. It was a long eight months and a hard journey from Division Hospital, in Petersburg, Virginia, to his deathbed in Candor. Meanwhile, the war had ended and President Lincoln had been assassinated, but John did not mention in his last brief letters that he knew or cared. He was hopeful of getting well, but finally applied for a pension in late July. What he most cared about toward the end was seeing Amelia one last time. John started his final letter to Amelia on October 13, 1865, with the plea, "Be sure to come without fail if you want to see me alive as soon as you get this letter." His pension had been approved only two months before his death, on October 17. He was 26 years old.

John was laid to rest in a cemetery near his sister's home. This cemetery, located on a small hill above North Candor Road, contains 65 graves. In recent years it has been known as the Snyder Station Cemetery, due to its proximity to a former railroad station of that name. The cemetery is not well maintained, but has large pine trees that limit undergrowth. A modest tombstone marks the site of John Tidd's burial.

While most Americans are exposed in school to American history, including the Civil War, they often do not know (and perhaps do not care) about the history of the places where they live and of the people who lived there before them, and of the events that took place there. The authors hope that by telling the story of an ordinary soldier, his friends and acquaintances, by blending their words and observations within a broader context, and by including relevant visual materials, we will honor those whose sacrifices saved the American Union from defeat and destruction.

John Tidd's grave at the Snyder Station Cemetery, near Candor, New York, 2010. Photograph by Mary Jordan.

Acknowledgments

THE AUTHORS OF *Dear Friend Amelia* are indebted to many people, without whom this completed work would not have been possible.

First and foremost, our sincere gratitude to Maggie Moesch for giving the Civil War letters to Mary.

Many thanks to the late Marian Gallagher and son Rodney Gallagher for permission to use letters from their personal collection, and to Alyce Mallett for family history and photographs. Thanks, too, are due Nancy and Ray Hunt of the Berkshire Historian's Office, who granted permission to use John Tidd's diary and additional letters and who offered research assistance. Also, we thank the U.S. Army Heritage and Education Center, Carlisle, Pennsylvania, for sharing additional letters from the Winey Collection.

Our heartfelt appreciation to Jill Swenson, who believed in us and our project. Her encouragement, guidance, and expertise was timely and critical to the success of our book.

We acknowledge with pleasure the enthusiasm of the board and staff of the Tioga County Historical Society (Owego, New York) who gave permission to use images from the Society's collection of Mathew Brady photographs.

We thank Dan Hill for graciously spending his valuable time with us imparting his vast Civil War knowledge. We also would like to extend our gratitude to Dorothy Torrey, who assisted with interviews and to John T. Goodnough, Binghamton Civil War Historical Society and Roundtable Secretary, Allen Chaffee, Newfield local historian, and Michael Colella, who shared their expertise, enthusiasm, extensive libraries, and collections.

Alan Littell generously read and gave the manuscript a thorough copy editing. Graphic designer Julie Manners offered many valuable suggestions regarding the layout of the book.

Additional thanks to Douglas Holleley and Edward Tufte for book design inspiration.

We thank the many readers of the manuscript who made helpful suggestions: Donna Eschenbrenner, Martin Sweeney, Carol Kammen, Chuck Geisler, Ian and Sarah Bailey, Emme Edmunds, Nancy Ostman, Patricia Fox, Kathy Morris, and Patty Buchanan.

We are grateful to Della Mancuso for shepherding *Dear Friend Amelia* through production.

Joyce's husband, Henry, always has encouraged us, believed in us, and afforded Joyce all the time she needed, for which we are eternally grateful.

This book has evolved during a lengthy ongoing process since John's letters were discovered in 1972. We may have overlooked mentioning persons who assisted us. Our sincere "Thank You" to all family and friends who encouraged us, prayed for us, and believed in us.

About the Authors

MARY JORDAN AND JOYCE HATCH are sisters who come from a large family born to Edna and Merritt Eggleston. They are middle daughters of 13 children. They share a love for history, especially that of rural central New York State, where they have lived their entire lives.

Mary has made her home in Speedsville for 47 years. She and husband, Donal, have two children and two grandchildren. Her *Pictorial History of Speedsville* is in its third edition. She collaborated with Paul Mitchell of Talbothay Books on the 1996 reprint edition of *Aunt Becky's Army-Life* (1867), revised to include an index, pictures, and a map of Sarah Palmer's (Becky's) travels while serving as a Civil War nurse for the 109th New York Volunteers. Mary is employed as an administrative assistant in the Department of Development Sociology at Cornell University.

Joyce and husband, Henry, reside in Groton. After being a stay-at-home mom, she was employed in office and managerial positions until launching a medical billing service in 1999. High on the Hatches' list of priorities are their four children, ten grandchildren, and their Christian faith.

Prior to joining Mary on *Dear Friend Amelia*, Joyce spent a number of years researching family genealogy, which included discovering a history of war veterans. Mary and Joyce's great grandfather fought in the Civil War in the 137th New York Volunteers and a great, great, great grandfather fought in the Revolutionary War.

Ronald E. Ostman is Emeritus Professor of Communication, Cornell University, Ithaca, New York, and has lived in upstate New York since 1979.

Harry Littell is publisher of Six Mile Creek Press, Ithaca, New York, and Chair of the Department of Photography at Tompkins Cortland Community College, Dryden, New York.

... dear boy it seems nearly as long
to you as it does to me, eight
day months have passed. and go
and still the war is not
ended but the prospect is get
brighter the day is breaking the
Southerners begin to tremble in
their shoes at the mighty power of the Government the Union
army is very strong and is gain-
strength every day, two or three
Regiments of deserters come back
every week under the Presidents
Procklimation, A. Mead has
come back to this company. the
came the first day of April
he was glad enough to get back
the news from Charleston to
day looks good, it is reported
that it was attacked last
Thursday and taken if it